714 2

Psych.

3
2
mol)

3

Beyond Relativism

Beyond Relativism reflects the current identity crisis in the social sciences. The relativist consensus, exemplified through the ascendancy of postmodernism, holds that knowledge and moral values are so embedded in concrete social and cultural settings that any objective account of either knowledge or morality has been rendered meaningless. This questions the relevance of the social sciences.

Raymond Boudon's theory of cognitive rationality represents a refreshing alternative to this view. Drawing on the assumption that mental contents and discourse are not completely shaped by society but rest on cognitive processes of active and reflexive subjects, his controversial approach suggests that social scientific knowledge is reducible neither to cultural and linguistic contexts nor to particular pragmatic interests. Can the theory of cognitive rationality simultaneously transcend relativism and overcome the limitations traditionally associated with methodological individualism?

Cynthia Lins Hamlin, in her challenging new work, persuasively argues that critical realism, by recognising both the agents' and social structure's causal powers and liabilities, offers the theory of cognitive rationality a powerful argument against the relativism that springs from the conflation of social reality and our ideas about it. *Beyond Relativism* is an important book for sociologists and for all those concerned with the methodology, and philosophy, of social science.

Cynthia Lins Hamlin is a lecturer in social theory at the Federal University of Pernambuco, Brazil. She is currently editor of the Brazilian journal *Estudos de Sociologia-Recife*.

Routledge Studies in Critical Realism
Edited by Margaret Archer, Roy Bhaskar, Andrew Collier,
Tony Lawson and Alan Norrie

Critical realism is one of the most influential developments in the philosophy of science and in the social sciences, providing a powerful alternative to positivism and postmodernism. The series will explore the critical realist position in philosophy and across the social sciences.

1   **Marxism and Realism**
    A materialistic application of realism in the social sciences
    Sean Craven

2   **Beyond Relativism**
    Raymond Boudon, cognitive rationality and critical realism
    Cynthia Lins Hamlin

Also published by Routledge:

Critical Realism: Interventions
Edited by Margaret Archer, Roy Bhaskar, Andrew Collier,
Tony Lawson and Alan Norrie

Critical Realism
Essential readings
*Edited by Margaret Archer, Roy Bhaskar, Andrew Collier, Tony Lawson
and Alan Norrie*

The Possibility of Naturalism, 3rd edition
A philosophical critique of the contemporary human sciences
Roy Bhaskar

Being and Worth
Andrew Collier

Quantum Theory and the Flight from Realism
Philosophical responses to quantum mechanics
Christopher Norris

From East to West
Odyssey of a soul
Roy Bhaskar

Realism and Racism
Concepts of race in sociological research
Bob Carter

Rational Choice Theory
Resisting colonisation
Edited by Margaret Archer and Jonathan Q Tritter

Explaining Society
An introduction to critical realism in the social sciences
*Berth Danermark, Mats Ekstrom, Jan Ch Karlsson and
Liselotte Kakobsen*

Critical Realism and Marxism
Edited by Andrew Brown, Steve Fleetwood and John Michael Roberts

Critical Realism in Economics
Edited by Steve Fleetwood

Realist Perspectives on Management and Organisation
Edited by Stephen Ackroyd and Steve Fleetwood

After International Relations
Critical realism and the (re)construction of world politics
Heikki Patomaki

Beyond Relativism

Raymond Boudon, cognitive rationality
and critical realism

Cynthia Lins Hamlin

London and New York

First published 2002
by Routledge
11 New Fetter Lane, London EC4P 4EE

Simultaneously published in the USA and Canada
by Routledge
29 West 35th Street, New York, NY 10001

Routledge is an imprint of the Taylor & Francis Group

Typeset in Sabon by
Prepress Projects Ltd, Perth, Scotland
Printed and bound in Great Britain by
TJ International Ltd, Padstow, Cornwall

British Library Cataloguing in Publication Data
A catalogue record for this book is available
from the British Library

Library of Congress Cataloging in Publication Data

Hamlin, Cynthia Lins, 1969–
  Beyond relativism: Raymond Boudon, cognitive rationality
and critical realism/Cynthia Lins Hamlin.
    p. cm. – (Routledge studies in critical realism ; 2)
Includes bibliographical references and index.
    1. Social psychology. 2. Social perception. 3. Cultural
relativism. 4. Cognition and culture. 5. Boudon, Raymond.
I. Title. II. Series.

HM1033 .H35 2001
302–dc21   2001048308

ISBN 0–415–25851–0

For Andy, Vozinho and Heraldo
In gratitude and admiration

Contents

Acknowledgements

I wish to express my immense gratitude to William Outhwaite, who supervised the thesis on which this book is based, and to my examiners, Michael Nicholson and Margaret Archer. I am especially indebted to Margaret Archer, for encouraging me to reformulate and submit the thesis for publication. Alan Norrie, Alan Jarvis and the anonymous Routledge referees provided helpful advice in the process of transforming the thesis into book form. Caroline New's detailed comments on the original manuscript were particularly helpful, and I fully acknowledge her insightful suggestions, which are too many to be listed here. A very special thank you goes to Raymond Boudon, who provided me with invaluable information on his work when interviewed and by generously supplying me with publications to which I would not otherwise have had access. Among those who have read and commented on particular sections of this book, I wish to thank Andrew Hamlin, José Maurício Domingues, Enzo Di Nuoscio, Luís Augusto de Gusmão, Verónica Tozzi, Silke Weber, Jorge Ventura de Morais and Josefa Salete Cavalcanti. My warmest thanks also go to Terry Mulhall, theory and language counsellor and a good friend, and last, but not least, to my family, for their love and support.

During the writing of both the thesis and the book I have received financial support from two Brazilian granting institutions linked to the Ministry of Education (CAPES) and to the Ministry of Science and Technology (CNPq). I have also received generous support from my colleagues in the Social Sciences Department at the Federal University of Pernambuco in Brazil.

Cynthia Lins Hamlin
August 2001

Introduction

This book is a defence of the social sciences against some of the relativist trends which have pervaded social thought. It will be of interest to anyone concerned with the main philosophical debates on the methodology of the social sciences, even though it is particularly directed to sociologists. This defence assumes the form of a critical reflection on the work of the French sociologist Raymond Boudon, informed by some of the contributions which critical realism has brought from philosophy into social theory and research.

This defence is both necessary and urgent. As Gerard Delanty (1997) has argued, the end of the twentieth century has witnessed the emergence of a new debate on the role of the social sciences. Different from the nineteenth century *fin de siécle*, the current debate has not dwelled upon the possibility or even the desirability of building a natural science of society, but on the usefulness of the social sciences in terms of their public influence, social impact and, ultimately, on their privileged status in relation to other forms of (non-specialised) knowledge.

This is, of course, part of a larger picture. The 'runaway world', to borrow Giddens' expression, has revealed in an unprecedented way the paradoxes of Enlightenment Reason. On the one hand, the 'natural world' is to such an extent transformed through human planning and manipulation that it is now virtually impossible to draw the line between the human and the natural world; Nature is a human creation as much as its own. On the other hand, processes such as global warming, the spread of microorganisms that are increasingly resistant to antibiotics and exposure of different species to plagues as a result of the rapid reduction of natural genetic libraries are only some of the signs of Nature's refusal to be put under control.

Such unintended consequences of human action upon Nature have also affected social relations in novel and unpredicted ways, contributing to the establishment of new forms of domination and social exclusion. It has, moreover, been generally accepted that it is not only our actions which have an impact on social reality, but also our theories. Information has been turned into another form of commodity, intensifying the effects of the double hermeneutics according to which specialised knowledge is constantly reinterpreted by social actors, sometimes working as self-fulfilling prophecies, sometimes merely providing a kind of cognitive context upon which social life is based.

This book does not intend to detail these processes, which have been described elsewhere by authors such as Delanty (1997) or Giddens (2000). Their function here is simply to illustrate the fact that, despite, and to a certain extent because of, the development of science, technology and specialised knowledge in general, both Nature and social life have increasingly challenged our forecasts and expectations, laying bare the frailty of our knowledge, but also revealing the social construction of a large portion of reality. *No . Reconstruction*

These consequences have had a major impact on philosophy and the social sciences. Notions such as objectivity and truth have become a favourite target of 'postmodern' thinkers and it has been largely assumed that scientific and philosophical discourse cannot be rendered more 'plausible', even though they may sometimes be more useful, than myths. This, of course, places a heavy burden on the shoulders of social scientists to the extent that their activity is not particularly justifiable. The core of the argument lies in the anti-realist thesis according to which knowledge is about constructed objects which have no real existence apart from the linguistic context in which they appear. According to constructivism, knowledge is both *moulded by* society and *about* society. Content is dissolved into context, and the choice between alternative accounts of reality becomes impossible (Bunge, 1999).

A second outcome of the aforementioned recognition is the idea that, if our descriptions of reality are incommensurable and can only be judged against particular pragmatic interests, then the values and beliefs which orient people's conduct are even less subject to rational evaluation, not to mention criticism. Like knowledge, values are taken to be so embedded in concrete social and cultural settings that there is no possibility of transcending them. Under the guise of relativism, all social demands are equally legitimate and all ideology is justifiable. In this sense, it is not only the positive or explanatory dimension of the social sciences which is put into question, but also their critical and normative role.

Raymond Boudon's work can be seen as a refreshing alternative to constructivism's relativism and scepticism. Critical of constructivism's idealism, his work postulates a certain degree of independence between social reality and our conceptions of it. Things exist independently of our knowledge of them and, within the limits of our capacities and resources, we can understand their nature and the process through which they came into being. Social phenomena, and this also includes all sorts of ideas, are not a mere reflection of culture and society; they are the result of people's ability to reason and the (intended and unintended) product of the actions of socially situated agents whose initiative, will and powers cannot be overlooked.

Boudon's anti-relativism has its source in a theory of human action whose main targets are represented by the different types of social/structural determinism which have dominated social theory, particularly French social theory, since Durkheim. Sociologism or 'social causalism' is considered by him, together with the totalising ambition of much of French structuralism, as one of the main causes of sociology's current crisis. It is with this in mind that he developed a neo-Weberian paradigm of social action, which culminated in his theory of cognitive rationality.

The theory of cognitive rationality brings Boudon close to a very 'un-French' tradition of thought, namely the utilitarian tradition represented by rational-choice theory. However, contrary to rational-choice theorists, Boudon does not assume that agents always act in terms of utility or preference maximisation, nor does he accept the idea that the preferences of agents (when they exist), their motives and their beliefs should be left unexplained. His theory of cognitive rationality can thus be seen not only as a theory of action, but also as a theory of beliefs (both positive and normative) which draws on the strong reasons that agents have for doing what they do or believing in what they believe.

One of the main differences between the theory of cognitive rationality and rational-choice theory lies in the former's assumption that it is contingent that strong reasons are objectively valid. Instrumental rationality, Boudon holds, is only a particular case of rationality, and a realistic model of the agents cannot rest on the abstract and calculating *Homo economicus*, but has to take into account their social and individual constitution, including affective, structural and other constraints and resources which bound and limit their cognitive abilities. This accounts for the fact that the beliefs of agents (including scientists) cannot always be clearly judged against reality or, in epistemological terms, that truth cannot always be known.

The epistemological relativism which follows from this model of the human agent does not, however, conflate the context of our knowledge with its content; individual mental contents and discourse are not completely shaped by society and, as the history of humankind has shown, it is in principle possible both to rebel against instituted ideas and to distinguish our constructs (concepts, theories, etc.) from reality. The most recent phase of Boudon's work is particularly aimed at the idea that these principles also apply to moral values, whose adherence rest on the same cognitive processes which ground other kinds of beliefs. This means that moral values are not simply a matter of social convention. They are cognitive ideas which refer to things and, because they present this property, they can be true or false, even though knowledge about them may sometimes be beyond our theories.

In formal terms, it is thus possible to agree with Alban Bouvier (1997) in identifying three closely related themes in Boudon's sociology: anti-determinism (or anti-causalism), anti-utilitarianism and anti-relativism. The first of these themes represents the leitmotif of his work insofar as it constitutes his response to the 'structuralist' tradition which has dominated French sociology since its establishment. However, Boudon's adherence to methodological individualism, which, together with the rationality principle, constitutes the pillar of his action paradigm, raises some problems for his theory of cognitive rationality and for social explanation in general.

Methodological individualism is considered by Boudon as an antidote to what he sometimes calls 'totalitarian realism': a foundationalist essentialism which mistakes the analysts' intellectual constructs (models, concepts and theories) for reality itself. It will be argued here that Boudon's arguments against essentialism, although they represent a sound concern, rest on a common misunderstanding which equates (social) realism with essentialism. Collective entities are taken by him to be conceptual constructs which should not be mistaken for reality itself, but since the same applies to the concept of individuals, he believes that this does not bear any direct consequences on social ontology. However, like most methodological individualists, he tends to oscillate between a (social) anti-realism and a weak realism with rationalist (neo-Kantian) overtones. The main consequence of this is a denial of the causal powers of social structures, which could lead Boudon to a reductionist theory of human agency, were not such powers implicitly included in his explanatory models. Such reductionism would, of course, jeopardise both the establishment of a socially situated agent and the distinction between individual mental contents and objective reality, the very axis of his anti-utilitarianism and his anti-relativism.

It will be shown that the adoption of an ontologically oriented realism, such as that developed by critical realists, which favours a multi-layered and emergent ontology, explicitly recognises the causal powers and liabilities of both the agents and the social structures. This allows for a better account of their properties and relations, thus avoiding any form of reductionism.

Despite being regarded as one of the most important contemporary sociologists, Boudon's work has not, in the Anglophone world, received the attention it deserves. In Chapter 1, particular attention will be devoted to the situation of his work within contemporary social science. Chapter 1 explores the background to his action paradigm, a background that has deep roots in an anti-essentialist social nominalism which opposes not realism, but idealism. The intent here consists in showing a certain elective affinity between nominalism, methodological individualism and a particular type of rationalism. This leads to a particular account of the notion of social structure and its relations to human agency.

The relations between structure and agency in Boudon's work will be examined in Chapter 2. It will be shown that the (explanatory) importance attributed to the notion of structure depends on the research problem which characterises each particular phase of his work. In this sense, Chapter 2 also constitutes a general overview of Boudon's main substantive interests. A certain tension between a 'situational analysis' and individualism can be noticed, especially in its structural form. This tension becomes particularly evident when nominalism is clearly reduced to its social variant. According to the general precepts of nominalism, it is necessary, in the process of concept and theory formation, to reject any form of essentialism. Sociological concepts are thus characterised as ideal types or models which bear a more or less adequate, but never a perfect, relation to reality. This adequacy, in its turn, is established through 'verification' procedures based on 'external' criteria, such as empirical observation (when possible), and on internal, non-empirical or rationalist ones, such as logical consistency and explanatory power.

It is possible to observe that, whereas reasons are considered as causes of actions, concepts and models relating to individuals can, in principle, be checked both at the external and the internal levels. The explanatory power of reasons follows from their characterisation in terms of necessary mechanisms for action, of underlying states or dispositions which are inherent to agents. In this sense, reasons are intrinsic to a particular type of object, and this can be known a priori, even though their adequacy (which reasons were causally efficacious in a particular course of action) can only be established a posteriori. The explanatory power of collective concepts and structural models, on the other hand, is limited by the fact that, contrary to reasons, social causes are not considered as truly explanatory, but as 'descriptive laws' which are always hard to establish. In a nutshell, the argument to be developed in Chapter 2 is that, whereas the reality of individual agents can be established both at the empirical and at the explanatory levels, the reality of collective entities cannot be established at either, because they are both unobservable, and their causal powers are not considered as such. The emphasis on the first pole of the agency–structure continuum is thus guaranteed by rendering social causes as mere methodological devices, as a 'methodological determinism', which would presumably help us to explain action by its inclusion in an extended notion of rationality.

The extended notion of rationality developed by Boudon can be seen as a critique to both those theories which reduce human reason to instrumental rationality, and to those which tend to portray human agents in terms of Garfinkel's 'cultural dopes'. The theory of cognitive rationality, investigated in Chapter 3, rests on a synthetic model of the social actor beyond the *Homo economicus* of positive economics and the *Homo sociologicus* of certain sociological approaches. This model of actor emphasises the social constitution of reasons, and the theory of cognitive rationality developed therefrom considers the social situation as both constraining and enabling, thus setting the limits and objective possibilities to action. Here it is possible to notice that the conception of individual agency adopted by Boudon is indeed very similar to the one adopted by critical realists, i.e. it rests on concepts such as purposefulness, intentionality and self-consciousness, all of which present an unavoidable social dimension. To a certain extent, this minimises the individualism which inheres in some of his methodological positions.

The main thesis of Boudon's theory of cognitive rationality can be roughly summarised as holding that the meaning of actions and beliefs can be understood when they rest on strong reasons, and reasons are strong when they rest on plausible conjectures. But in order to avoid the simplistic conclusion that all strong reasons are objectively valid, which would reduce rationality to instrumental rationality, Boudon needs to be able to differentiate between the agents' accounts of reality and objective reality.

This problem is strictly linked to the nature of social explanation and its relation to understanding and interpretation, which constitutes the subject of Chapter 4. Here, particular attention is paid to the problem of causality and causal explanation in the social sciences, and how this relates to the understanding of reasons and the interpretation of the symbolic framework which helps agents to reproduce and/or transform social reality. The core of the argument to be developed here is that, because he lacks a unified notion of causality which would enable him to deal with both the agency and the structural aspects of social explanation, Boudon oscillates instead between a rationalist notion of causality, a straightforward Humean one, and Donald Davidson's modification of the latter. A realist critique of the aforementioned notions of causality demonstrates why it is difficult for the theory of cognitive rationality both to adequately grasp the relations between social structure and individual agency, and to establish itself as an objective account of social phenomena.

Boudon's theory of cognitive rationality, which springs from his paradigm of social action, is characterised here as a pendular movement between the antinomies generated by the combination of a social nominalism and a form of realism of rationalist undertones. To the extent that Boudon wants to explain the beliefs and values which ground (rational) action, the pendulum moves towards realism given the need to establish the adequacy of the structural models developed with that purpose. The more it moves in that direction, the more difficult it is to sustain his idea that structural causes constitute only a 'methodological determinism', rather than real causal forces. Just as the causal adequacy of reasons can be justified with the aid of non-empirical criteria, so also can the adequacy of structural ones. In this sense, the main thesis to be defended here is that the explicit adoption of a non-empiricist ontology provides a sounder basis for Boudon's theory of cognitive rationality, characterising it as a more powerful tool in the defence of sociology's positive and normative roles.

1 The action paradigm

Bringing the agent back in

Raymond Boudon was born in Paris in 1934 and, together with Michel Crozier, Alain Touraine and Pierre Bourdieu, he is part of the second generation of French sociologists who have helped to establish sociology as an academic discipline (Bell, 1998). Often praised for the clarity of his style and the extensive use of illustrative examples, Boudon is the author of a vast body of work whose main themes include education, social stratification and social mobility; the sociology of knowledge and the philosophy of the social sciences; classical social theory and, more recently, human values. This 'thematic nomadism' can largely be rendered responsible for the constant attention his work has attracted world-wide, placing him among the most important contemporary sociologists.

The wide thematic span of Boudon's work has allowed him to make important contributions in virtually all the areas traditionally dealt with by sociology, but if one has to single out his most enduring contribution to the social sciences, this would no doubt refer to his critique of the many traditions which neglected the role of human agency in social phenomena. Boudon shares with the aforementioned authors of his generation a great concern with the 'death of the subject' announced by the previously dominant structuralist tradition which, in France, was based on the works of Althusser, Lévi-Strauss, Foucault and Lacan. Even though structuralism does not represent a homogeneous project, it is possible to identify a common trend, namely the idea that human agency is the effect of the social structure. In more contemporary terms, this critique has been translated into a refusal to comply with a widespread constructivism which, influenced by the idealistic wing of structuralism, phenomenology, post-structuralism, deconstructionism, etc., conflates human practice and discourse.

The general reaction against structuralism undertaken by Boudon, Crozier, Touraine and Bourdieu has generated different accounts of human agency and its relation to the social context in which it occurs. In this sense, a good introduction to Boudon's specific approach is a brief comparison between these authors' response to the structuralist tradition. Starting with Michel Crozier, his strategic analysis rejects any structural or social determinism by establishing that social systems constrain, but do not determine, the behaviour of agents. They represent instead structured games whose rules are 'open' enough for agents to maintain a certain degree of autonomy, particularly in interpreting their roles and defining strategies. These 'zones of uncertainty' constitute an important source of power to the extent that the power which an actor has over another largely depends on the unpredictable character of his or her behaviour (Durand and Weil, 1990). In this sense, agents are always negotiating their freedom and the zones of uncertainty that it engenders, and power relations are taken to represent the main source of social change and/or reproduction. This means that, for Crozier, social systems are not the deterministic result of any laws, but the (contingent) consequence of the power relations between agents within a particular system.

Beyond their differences, the importance of human agency is also taken into account by Touraine, Bourdieu and Boudon, even though Boudon is rather sceptical about the centrality accorded to the notion of power in Crozier's analyses, arguing that it assumes the status of a unique mechanism of social change (Boudon and Bourricaud, 1982). Boudon rejects any quest for a *primum movens* or for causal monism when it comes to explaining social phenomena, whether the causes in question refer to social conflict, to ideas or to values. This is why he criticises the centrality accorded to concepts such as power and class in defining historical agents, and this can also be considered as one of the main sources of difference between him, on the one hand, and Touraine and Bourdieu, on the other.

Despite Touraine's rejection of both individualism and the emphasis on the strategic dimension of human behaviour, which marks a strong difference between him and Boudon, he also rejects the common representation of social life in the 1960s which 'left no room for social actors' (Touraine, 1988: xxii). For Boudon, however, the problem with Touraine is not so much his anti-individualistic conception of the social agent, for he thinks it is possible to speak of collective agency, but Touraine's conception of history, which he takes to be the result of an immanent sense of history in minds of individuals, as if history had its own telos (Boudon and Bourricaud, 1982; Boudon, 1984). This, in its turn, would lead to the impossibility of transcending structuralism's social and cultural determinism to the extent that the values and beliefs of agents would reflect in an almost mechanical way the interests of dominant groups.

His differences with Bourdieu in this matter are still greater, even though they have some important aspects of their general projects in common. In the first place, both authors' work can be characterised as a synthetic enterprise which tries to overcome certain dualisms such as subjectivism–objectivism, agency–structure, etc. In particular, both criticise Althusser's philosophical version of structuralism, according to which social agents are mere bearers of the social structure; both criticise Lévi-Strauss' anthropological structuralism, which, drawing on Saussure's linguistic model, leads to a conception of practices in terms of a mechanical adoption of rules and models; finally, both criticise the totalising ambition of philosophy, without agreeing with most of the atheoretical analyses which characterise the sociological empirical tradition. However, their responses to each of these problems take different, if not opposed, routes. Boudon often emphasises Bourdieu's 'structuralism', given his inability to explain the origins of *habitus*, that is, of the dispositions of agents to act in particular ways, arguing that, according to the latter, *habitus* is fully determined by the agents' position in the stratification system (see Boudon, 1986a; 1999a).

The aforementioned criticism is closely linked to Boudon's rejection of 'irrationalism', which ultimately refers to the rather carefree manner in which Bourdieu and others, drawing on the works of 'the masters of suspicion' (Freud, Marx and Nietzsche), make recourse to obscure forces which act behind the back of the agents. Although Boudon does not deny the causal influence of 'irrational causes', these forces are taken to be sometimes overrated, whether they refer to unconscious mechanisms, as in Freud, to alienation, as in Marx, or to a basic and largely unconscious social structure, as in Lévi-Strauss (Godbout, 1996).

Structuralism and Marxism (especially as informed by the former) are thus viewed as dogmatic frameworks which, in the name of tradition (that of the French 1968 generation), reject heterodox questions and explanations. Boudon's critique of these approaches can, for the sake of analogy, be compared to Derrida's attempt to deconstruct fixed ideas on the basis that much of our preconceived ideas rest on the exclusion of difference. However, contrary to deconstructionism's plea for the abandonment of a quest for reconstruction, Boudon sustains that sociology is not a mere rhetorical or aesthetic activity and its first rule is to attempt to build controllable statements which can help us to understand social phenomena better. This places him against another type of dogmatism: that of sceptics and pluralists who conceive scientific theories as 'just a heap of inscriptions' (Bunge, 1999: 178).

Cautious as to the limits of scientific knowledge to adequately grasp reality, Boudon's work can also be located in relation to what he terms 'the new sociology of knowledge', a wide terminology which includes the Edinburgh 'strong programme' and authors such as Bruno Latour and Kurt Hübner. With his characteristic style, described by one of his critics as showing a tendency towards qualifying and limiting other people's assumptions rather than demolishing them, Boudon agrees that knowledge can only arise out of particular frameworks according to which reality is perceived and interpreted, but the lack of absolute or foundationalist principles does not prevent rational evaluation (Boudon, 1990a; 1995a; 1999a; 2000). What is at stake here is the denial that truth is basically a social construction (although it is socially discovered) and also that the social system completely determines our mental contents, abilities, dispositions and discourse. As in other aspects of social life, human beings have to be conceived as agents who have the ability to reason and to change the current state of affairs through their actions, and this power to change things cannot always be dissociated from the agents' ability to adequately grasp reality.

This focus on the active and reflexive character of human beings rests on the privileged role attributed to human reason in the explanation of social phenomena, an assumption equally shared by rational-choice theorists. However, contrary to the utilitarian tradition which informs authors like Gary Becker, for instance, Boudon does not identify human beings with a bundle of interests, nor does he conceive human practice in terms of utility maximisation. Society is much wider than the economic sphere, and extending that domain to the whole of social relations leads to a very unrealistic conception of the human agent and of social relations. At the same time, he does not agree with Jon Elster's arguments in favour of a thin definition of rationality, i.e. a definition based on the means–end scheme. Rationality is, for him, a very wide notion which cannot be established a priori for it is intrinsically linked to the social context in which the action occurs: 'as all evaluative notions, truth and rationality are "ordinal", not "cardinal"; comparative, not absolute notions' (Boudon, forthcoming). This extended conception of rationality allows him to extend the concept to domains which are normally outside the scope of rational-choice theory, such as the explanation of moral beliefs. The latter are neither based on the notion of exchange, nor on the pursuit of certain ends, but on the agents' ability to act according to basic principles of social organisation which can be rendered 'rational'. The theory of cognitive rationality which springs from his critique of both social determinism and of rational-choice theory can be considered as a synthesis of Boudon's contributions to the social sciences.

This general and non-exhaustive situation of Boudon's thought aims to show the centrality accorded by him to the notion of action and the consequent denial that human beings can be treated as mere puppets, as if they were completely controlled by 'external' or hidden forces that obey their own logic. Although the problem is no longer put in terms of a Kantian opposition between Reason and Nature, autonomy is still seen as a fundamental element in the characterisation of what being human means, and human agency is seen as an important causal force in the reproduction and transformation of social systems. This general concern with the role of human agency in social phenomena has led him to develop a paradigm of social action as a response to structuralism's determinist and irrationalist trends, based on the distinction between interactionist and determinist paradigms.

Interactionist and determinist paradigms of action

According to Boudon (1980: 308), the difference between an individualistic explanation and a collectivist one is that, whereas the latter is based on the establishment of a causal relation between a phenomenon P and another P' (i.e. P'→P), the former considers the phenomenon P as a consequence of the actions of individuals under conditions P'. This difference is also put in terms of two paradigm families: interactionist and determinist.

Although the characterisation of interactionist paradigms was originally made on the basis of a rather utilitarian conception of agency which is no longer sustained by Boudon, the distinction between those two families assumes a central importance throughout his work: interactionist paradigms guide those sociological theories whose language suggests 'that the social phenomenon to be explained is produced by the juxtaposition or by the composition of a set of actions' (Boudon, 1982: 156). Determinist paradigms, on the other hand, are those in which 'acts are always explained in terms of elements prior to these acts' (ibid.: 157).[1] For Boudon, there are four major types of interactionist paradigms: Marxian, Tocquevillian, Mertonian and Weberian, and the differences between them rest on the kinds of elements which are considered relevant for the understanding of action. These elements may refer to macro-structures, institutions, role-sets, socialisation, cognitive structures, etc.

In Marxian paradigms, individual actions are taken to be 'unrelated' in two senses: the agent performs them without having to consider their effects on others (they happen in a 'state of nature'), and preferences are considered as obvious, thus assuming the status of independent variables.[2] For Boudon, Marx is 'the sociologist who most consistently interpreted social change as the result of effects of composition. He posits social agents exclusively preoccupied with the pursuit of immediately decipherable interests in which they are free to disregard the effect of their action on others' (ibid.: 166). Although this very utilitarian conception of Marx's work has been the target of many criticisms (see Durand and Weil, 1980; Favre, 1980), its general conception of explanation is still maintained by Boudon as a possible one.

Tocquevillian paradigms are those in which choices are made in a state of nature, and systems of preferences are not self evident, having to be explained in terms of the social system to which they belong. The difference between Marxian and Tocquevillian paradigms rests on the more or less evident character of actors' preference systems and whether, according to research aims, they have to be explained:

> The distinction between these two types [of paradigms] has nothing to do with the distinction (to me a confused one and anyway of little use here) between the different ways in which individual preferences may be determined (for instance determination by social structures and determination by human nature).
>
> (Boudon, 1982: 177)

This suggests that, in Tocquevillian paradigms, social structures are important to the extent that structural constraints and enabling conditions allow for the possible outcomes (and not determination) of action. Social structures are taken to limit the options open to the agents and to determine the relative value of choices, but not the choices themselves. When preferences are viewed as a direct product of social structures, there is a reduction of Tocquevillian paradigms to what Boudon calls 'totalitarian realism', i.e. a 'deterministic' paradigm in which choices are the apparent product of chosen ends and the real product of structural determinism.

Paradigms of the Mertonian type are defined in terms of three main features:

1   The actions studied arise in a context of contract, i.e. the notion of role is fundamental to the extent that it refers to the actors' more or less explicit commitments.
2   These actions, as in the preceding case, also obey the principle of the pursuit of individual interest.
3   Preferences, or rather the way in which they emerge, can be considered either as self-evident or in need of explanation.

Boudon considers that, although the notion of role restricts the margin of individual autonomy, it does not determine action. This is because the social position of an individual is described, as by Merton, in terms of the multiple roles that he or she assumes (status-set) and 'the different types of relations and the diversity of roles that characterise the individual's position in each institution' (role-set) (Boudon, 1982: 185). The variability, multiplicity and individual complexity of roles give the actor leeway for interpretation (of their own and of other people's roles). In other words, as in Crozier's analyses, 'roles are thought of as guides to action. But these guides always offer a margin of indeterminacy' (ibid.: 193). Boudon calls the determinist version of Mertonian paradigms 'hyperfunctionalist paradigms', and they rest on the assumptions that:

> (1) Every action arises in a 'contractual' context (in other words, no action arises in a 'state of nature' context); (2) role-sets and status-sets are composed of complementary and non-contradictory elements; (3) the leeway for interpretation of the elements in the role-sets and status-sets is either non-existent or of no real interest.
>
> (ibid.)

A basic feature of Weberian paradigms is that certain elements of action, such as the structuring of systems of preferences, choices of the appropriate means, etc., must be analysed in terms of some other non-trivial elements which preceded that action. These non-trivial elements refer not only to structural, but also to cognitive, affective, traditional factors, etc. According to Boudon, in Weber's work, action can either take place in a state of nature or in a contract context, and trivial preferences can appear either as dependent or as independent variables. The consideration of one or another element in the analysis depends on the phenomenon to be explained. The reductionist versions of Weberian paradigms, i.e. the explanation of action solely in terms of elements prior to it, are called 'hyperculturalist paradigms'.

Despite the variation in the consideration of elements prior to action, all interactionist paradigms have in common the fact that action is not a mechanical consequence of those elements. In addition to that, they consider that the social structure which results from the aggregation of actions is, in principle, reducible to those actions. It seems, however, that the particular type of structure which springs from an individualistic analysis only affects the definition of the structure to be explained, since it presupposes a previous one. This social structure which is presupposed, although it can be further analysed in terms of the aggregation of previous social actions, is described in terms of very general features which can be characterised as ideal types, for it does not entail a realistic description of the context. As with Weberian ideal types, it involves a selection of elements which are considered relevant to the explanation in question and which depend basically on the kind of problem proposed or on the phenomenon to be explained.

These general characteristics are then summarised in what Boudon terms the neo-Weberian paradigm, according to which the explanation of a social phenomenon 'M' is to:

1   Treat M as the result of the aggregation of a set of individual actions. In formal terms, 'M is a function $M(m_i, m_j)$ of the behaviour m_i of actors belonging to the category i and of the behaviour m_j of actors j (supposing it is necessary to distinguish the two social categories i and j); $M = M(m_i, m_j)$.'

2   Show that these actions are understandable, given the situation in which the actors are (S_i for the former, S_j for the latter). 'In a nutshell, the behaviour m_i should be considered a function of the Situation S_i and m_j as a function of S_j: $m_i = m_i(S_i)$ and $m_j = m_j(S_j)$'.

3   Show that, in most cases, the Situation S_i is a result of a factor P which belongs to the social system or to a level which is 'above' the individual: '$S_i = S_i(P_i)$ and $S_j = S_j(P_j)$'. In summary, the equation which represents Boudon's paradigm of action is $M = M\{m[S(P)]\}$. (Boudon, 1989b: 242).[3]

For Boudon, this model differs from the 'covering law' model of explanation insofar as it does not presuppose the idea of social or psychological laws. On the contrary, what is at stake is a kind of 'projective postulate' according to which I can put myself into someone else's shoes whenever I have sufficient information and conclude that, had I been in the same position, I would have acted in the same way (Boudon, 1989b: 242). In this sense, the character of the social sciences is not nomothetic, but formal. By formal he means based on models and, in a characteristically neo-Kantian argument, formal (or ideal) models alone do not allow for any empirical conclusion about reality, unless the terms involved are defined in a precise way.

The generality of models cannot be confused with the idea of general laws. A formal model is general only in the sense that it is applicable to many situations insofar as it is complemented by the appropriate information.

For Boudon, the notion of a model is the modern equivalent of the Weberian notion of ideal type and the Simmelian notion of formal sociology. These two notions constitute the basis of their nominalist or anti-essentialist sociology, that is, a sociology which emphasises the difference between schemes of intelligibility built by the observer and reality itself. These schemes of intelligibility presuppose an extreme simplification of reality:

> [W]e shall not take into account the individuals who are actually responsible for M in their concrete individuality, but we shall classify them in general categories. We shall not take into account all the traits belonging to the social system, but only a small number of them which shall suffice for the explanation. In short, we shall build a simplifying model in order to explain a reality which is generally complex.
>
> (Boudon, 1989b: 243)[4]

This distinction between schemes of intelligibility and reality provides the basis for the epistemological and methodological principles guiding Boudon's paradigm of action, which can also be understood in terms of two closely related propositions shared by Weber and Popper: methodological individualism and a rationality principle.

Methodological individualism is considered as a principle which states that, in order 'to explain a social phenomenon ... it is necessary to reconstruct the motivations of the individuals involved in the phenomenon in question and to apprehend that phenomenon as the result of the aggregation of the individual behaviours dictated by those motivations' (Boudon 1986c: 46).[5] The rationality principle, in its turn, is considered as a heuristic model which postulates a certain degree of autonomy to social agents by rendering them 'rational' or, in other words, that, more often than not, individuals have 'good reasons' for believing in what they believe and for acting as they do in a given context or situation. The rationality principle is often described as 'the Weber–Popper postulate', and it constitutes the central axis of Boudon's methodological prescriptions.

According to the formal characterisation of Boudon's sociology, these principles are not to be considered as ontological claims, but as methodological rules which spring from a rationalist epistemology that provides a link between nominalism and individualism.

Nominalism, rationalism and individualism

In order to show the specific contour of Boudon's paradigm of action, I shall now try to reconstruct it on the basis of a particular tradition of thought, namely a nominalist one, shared by Popper, Weber, Simmel and Boudon's former teacher and co-worker, Paul Lazarsfeld. The aim of this reconstruction is to show how methodological individualism is, in Boudon's view, the result of a rationalist or non-empiricist epistemology, presenting a methodological rather than an ontological status. This characterisation of methodological individualism as a methodological or explanatory approach would allow for a clear-cut differentiation between individualism, or the idea that the explanation has to refer to the contents of an individual's mind, such as motives, beliefs, etc., and atomism, or the thesis according to which only individuals (the atoms of social analysis) are real entities, capable of generating real effects on reality. As it will become evident, this distinction is very problematic for methodological individualists and, although Boudon sometimes describes methodological individualism in atomistic terms, he also makes a great effort to differentiate the two approaches by means of a rationalist epistemology according to which the correspondence between concepts, models, theories and reality cannot be judged on empirical criteria alone.

For Boudon (1996c), it does not make sense to deny the existence of collective entities, and methodological individualism should not be considered as a defence of such a view. In fact, he advocates that such ontological questions tend to be naïve, leading us nowhere. Like many classical individualists, such as Popper, Hayek and Schumpeter, he believes sociologists can and should exclude any metaphysical and ontological questions from their domains. But this position is by no means universal among methodological individualists: Dario Antisseri, Enzo Di Nuoscio, David Bidney and Luciano Pellicani believe that the ontological status of culture and social institutions is a problem which the empirical social sciences cannot ignore (see Antisseri and Pellicani, 1992; Di Nuoscio, 1996). As this internal split suggests, any characterisation of methodological individualism has to take the differences between ontology and methodology into account.

Although methodological individualism has its roots in classical and neo-classical economics, on the one hand, and in British empiricism, on the other, it is also possible to trace the debate over the status of individuals and social structures to an older debate between nominalists and realists in scholastic philosophy. Nominalism is a notion often associated with individualism and, in its strictest sense, it states that only names or words are universal, whereas all the things named are singular. Nature, according to this view, consists of atomistic or singular things and events, and the only things they can have in common are names. In the development of the aforementioned debate, it became accepted by both sides that there are qualities which are general and which transcend individual objects (such as the colour red, for instance). This means that both parties accepted a realist definition of universals. However, nominalists denied that any universals are real. It was therefore over the notion of reality, especially in the way that this notion was articulated progressively by Descartes, Hume and Kant in modern philosophy, that nominalism retained its strength and pervaded a great part of the social sciences (Lewis and Smith, 1980).

According to Lewis and Smith (ibid.: 14), these philosophical systems 'approach ontology through epistemology by reducing the question "what is there?" to the question "what can be known?"'. In particular, they showed that the sensorial qualities of the objects perceived are always mediated through the human mind, i.e. perception depends on the structure of our sensory organs and on cognitive factors. But once ontology was put aside in favour of epistemology, it was epistemology which determined what was admitted into ontology (Outhwaite, 1987). This means that even though ontology may not be at the centre of someone's concerns, the separation between theory, methodology and ontology is not an absolute one: social ontology, be it in the form of a priori commitments or of consequences of successful explanatory strategies, does have epistemological, methodological and theoretical import for the simple fact that there is an unavoidable link between what something is held to be and how it should be conceptualised and explained (and vice versa) (Bhargava, 1992; Archer, 1995).

Given this, it is possible to infer a particular ontology from the epistemological positions defended by modern philosophy. In particular, as Roy Bhaskar has shown, the hegemonic position of the empiricist tradition led to the identification of being and perception, and the ontology which can be derived from this position is entirely based on the possibility of observing certain characteristics of the objects of experience, i.e. atomistic events and the constant conjunctions between them (Bhaskar, 1997).

This atomistic ontology is often associated with a general misconception which equates singular objects with human individuals, on the one hand, and general properties with social structures, on the other. It is thus only natural that nominalism in the social sciences became identified with a general social ontology whose problematic is essentially a question of 'whether social reality is to be reduced to properties of individuals and their relationships (social nominalism), or, alternatively, whether there are also characteristics of collective units not fully definable and explicable in terms of the properties of the individuals comprising them (social realism)' (Lewis and Smith, 1980: 8).

Boudon's defence of nominalism can be seen in two related arguments. The most widespread one refers to 'totalitarian realism', which in social theory is taken to mean that individual behaviour is completely determined by the social structure (Boudon, 1982). Another reference to nominalism can be found in his early works with Paul Lazarsfeld (Boudon and Lazarsfeld, 1965), characterising a critique of the positivist belief (of logical empiricism) that it was possible to build concepts and theories solely by observing reality. Generally speaking, this critique constituted a denial of the radical reduction of being to experience about being.

According to logical positivism, knowledge can only be based on experience and, since it is impossible to observe general things, knowledge can only refer to individual objects and their constant conjunctions. This led to an attempt to build science's vocabulary in terms of theoretical concepts which could be reduced to observational statements, that is, general concepts could be used only if they could be reduced to singular ones, defined in terms of singular things which presented a particular location within time and space. Boudon's and Lazarsfeld's central thesis against this view was taken from the linguistic turn according to which concepts do not have any meaning when taken in isolation, for meaning is part of a theoretical structure which has to be considered as a whole. In this sense, more important than finding empirical referents to concepts used by scientists is the precise building of the theoretical structures in which concepts are combined. This is in fact a very powerful idea which, by denying an identity between concepts and observable reality, also denies (a linguistic) essentialism or, what for them is often considered as the same thing, realism.

Given the epistemological focus of their work, nominalism is considered as a methodological, and not an ontological, approach. Lazarsfeld, for instance, who was particularly concerned with building a precise and non-ambiguous vocabulary for the social sciences, defined nominalism as an approach which analyses the concepts used by scientists in scientific discourse only. This constitutes the core of his methodology, known as *explication de texte*. In this procedure, he identifies the current uses of a term in different traditions and specifies its meaning according to common dimensions (or aspects) hidden under terminological differences. A good example is the analysis of the concept of attitude:

> We shall see that the definition given for the concept 'attitude' is no longer concerned with its correspondence with the current notion of the term; rather, it succeeds in identifying, in terms of research language, a scientific object with specific characteristics (unobservability, intentionality, polarity ...). This is the important point: observability implies the use of special inference techniques, intentionality presupposes a verbal or real stimulus, etc. Thus, what is identified behind the term attitude is a specific scientific *démarche*. The name itself matters little: 'disposition', 'feeling', would be as justifiable.
>
> (Stoetzel and Lazarsfeld, 1965: 189)[6]

In a strict sense, the idea that the meaning of a concept refers to a specific scientific *démarche* is an expression of operationalism (the meaning of theoretical terms is identified with the operations used in their measurement). Although, for reasons which I cannot develop here, Lazarsfeld did not strictly subscribe to operationalism, he could not escape a somewhat attenuated version of this doctrine, instrumentalism. According to the basic instrumentalist postulate, since our senses cannot verify any claims about unobservable entities, theories about such things cannot be considered as anything more than 'instruments' for ordering and summarising observational claims (Papineau, 1978: 26).

Both operationalism and instrumentalism hold on to the idea that since a tool, unlike a statement, does not really say anything about reality, then it does not matter which words or concepts are used, but only what is 'behind' them (dimensions, aspects or components). In Lazarsfeld's case this has a direct bearing on *social* nominalism. Instrumentalism is a nominalist or an anti-realist approach to the extent that concepts can only be considered as fictions which are more or less useful, not true or false (Hamlin, 2000a). Although this should apply to all concepts used by social scientists, it may lead to *social* nominalism insofar as the dimensions, aspects or components of (collective) concepts are to be reduced, whenever possible, to observational statements (individual persons): 'propositions about collectives are sometimes made as substitutes for propositions about individual persons, simply because the necessary data about individual persons are not available' (Lazarsfeld, 1993: 175).

Boudon does not agree with such reductionism, for he recognises the fact that most concepts relating to individuals are also non-observable. He argues that, despite Lazarsfeld's empiricist prescriptions, his substantive works are inscribed into what he calls the *Verstehen* tradition, which summarises the two postulates mentioned earlier:

> Postulate 1: social phenomena are the product of actions, attitudes, individual beliefs; the former result from their aggregation. ...
> Postulate 2: explaining these actions means rendering them understandable. That is to say, the sociologist must find the meanings those actions, beliefs or attitudes had for the social actors themselves. More precisely, given that the notion of meaning is not perfectly clear, the sociologist must find the reasons which lead (or led) the actor to do X, believe (or have believed) that Y is true, good, etc.
> (Boudon, 1997b: 2)[7]

According to him, behind Lazarsfeld's nominalist quotes one simply finds the idea that social facts always involve human beings and their attitudes, beliefs, and so on (Boudon 1996b). In this sense, nominalism is not really taken to be based on reductionism, but it is aimed against essentialism or the view according to which our concepts describe the 'essence' of phenomena. For Boudon, contrary to Lazarsfeld's empiricist bias, the social structure is not just a residual concept arising out of the impossibility of reducing collectives (non-observables) to individuals (observables), but it has to be taken into account in a 'situational analysis' which accounts for the socially indexed character of the social actor. Situational analysis was developed by Karl Popper and, together with the rationality principle which is linked to it, constitutes one of the pillars of Boudon's action paradigm.

In Popper's work, situational analysis springs directly from his thesis of the unity of scientific method. According to this thesis, the hypothetico-deductive model is the only possible way of 'testing' hypotheses and constructing scientific theories. The main argument behind this method is that there is no such thing as knowledge by induction from repetition, because the human mind has inborn dispositions to knowledge which are modified throughout time. Those dispositions which are not inborn or later modifications of them are taken from objective knowledge, based on rationality, and not on experiences which are impressed on the mind as such. Against empiricism's view, experiences are always, in some sense, selected, interpreted and modified (Popper, 1994).

Popper's distinction between deductivism and inductivism substantially overlaps with the classical distinction between rationalism and empiricism: whereas empiricism is based on the idea that science proceeds by collecting observations which are then inductively generalised, rationalism rests on the idea that there are some self-evident principles, based on reason, from which it is possible to deduce certain statements about the world.[8] But Popper's rationalist approach is distinct in that it refers mainly to the process of theory 'testing'. It represents a 'weak rationalism', in the sense that it merely points to the theory laden aspect of experience. First, it has to be distinguished from Kant's notion that those self-evident principles are synthetic and a priori: for Popper, they are conjectures or hypotheses. In addition to that, these conjectures or hypotheses are not mere instruments or definitions which cannot be subject to empirical testing: 'They are therefore synthetic (rather than analytic); empirical (rather than a priori); informative (rather than purely instrumental)' (Popper, 1957: 132).

How these hypotheses are arrived at is, for Popper, a matter of individual psychology. The process is not part of the logical process of science, since it is not generated according to critical rationalist principles; it rests outside methodology. There is thus a sharp distinction between 'the process of conceiving a new idea, and the methods and results of examining it logically'(Popper, 1965: 31). This, along with Popper's emphasis on empirical criteria of theory testing, represents an important source of difference between him and Boudon. As we shall have the chance to observe, the Weberian method called *Verstehen* has a very important role in concept and model formation and, in this sense, these problems assume a central position in Boudon's methodology.

According to Popper, the rational aspect of science is guaranteed through the possibility of testing hypotheses, not of 'scientifically' generating them. Moreover, contrary to the claims of logical empiricists, the demarcation criterion which allows us to differentiate between science and metaphysics is not an inductivist one based on the possibility of logical reduction of universal statements to elementary statements of experience (verifiability). For Popper, such reduction is not possible because the former are never derivable from singular statements (and this constitutes an important argument shared by Popper and Boudon against considering methodological individualism as an empiricist and reductionist approach). Popper's demarcation criterion rests, rather, on an asymmetry between verifiability and falsifiability, i.e. on the idea that, although universal statements cannot be derivable from singular ones, they can be contradicted or falsified by the latter. In other words, he believes that it is possible to argue from the truth of singular statements to the falsity of universal ones by means of purely deductive inferences: the observation of a single black swan would be enough to falsify the general statement 'all swans are white'.

In this way Popper claims to have solved the Humean problem of induction concerning the validity of natural laws. Although this problem shall not concern me here, it is important to emphasise that Popper's anti-atomism rests on the argument that there can be no sharp distinction between pure observational generalisations and more abstract laws or theories. Almost every statement transcends experience: universal laws because they transcend any finite number of observable instances; singular statements because they incorporate universal terms and these are dispositional words, i.e. they are words which characterise the law-like behaviour of certain things. In this sense, 'universal laws transcend experience in at least two ways: because of their universality, and because of the occurrence of universal or dispositional terms in them' (Popper, 1965: 425). Universal laws, as well as theories, singular statements concerning 'facts', etc., can never be empirically verified: they can only be contradicted by our experiences. For this reason, explanation cannot rest on the reduction of general to individual things, but on a 'methodological nominalism' which takes seriously the gap between concepts and models, on the one hand, and reality, on the other.

Referring back to the scholastic debate over the (ontological) status of universals, Popper (1957) argues that the traditional opposition to the nominalist view according to which universals differ from singular names only by virtue of their being applied to sets or classes of single things, rather than to one single thing, has been called both realism and idealism. For him, applying the term realism to the scholastic anti-nominalist party is most misleading. Therefore, he proposes to call it 'essentialism' instead, and defines his own position as realism, meaning that some of the entities which science describes are real.

According to scholastic essentialism, the properties denoted by universal terms were considered universal objects or 'essences' which have an ontological status. In a somewhat different strand, what Popper calls 'methodological essentialists' avoid the ontological dimension of universals, concentrating instead on the ends and means of science, i.e. on methodological issues. This school, founded by Aristotle, considers that the aim of science is to reveal the essences of things and describe them by means of concepts or definitions. Against this methodological essentialism, Popper (1947: 26) introduces his own position, calling it 'methodological nominalism'. The differences between the two methodologies can be described as follows:

> Methodological essentialists are inclined to formulate scientific questions in such terms as 'what is matter?' or 'what is force?' or 'what is justice?' and they believe that a penetrating answer to such questions, revealing the real or essential meaning of these terms and thereby the real or true

nature of the essences denoted by them, is at least a necessary prerequisite of scientific research, if not its main task. Methodological nominalists, as opposed to this, would put their problems in such terms as 'how does this piece of matter behave?' or 'how does it move in the presence of other bodies?'. For methodological nominalists hold that the task of science is only to describe how things behave, and suggest that this is to be done by freely introducing new terms wherever necessary, or by re-defining old terms wherever convenient while cheerfully neglecting their original meaning. For they regard words merely as useful instruments of description.

(Popper, 1947: 29)

As with Lazarsfeld's methodological prescriptions, one finds a certain degree of instrumentalism in this passage. For Popper, hypotheses are models which can be falsified, but never verified, and should not be mistaken for concrete things. Although it is certainly true that concepts are not concrete things, they must refer (if they are to play a role in explanation at all) to things that really exist. By saying that a concept provides a proper description of objects and their dispositional properties, one is also saying that those properties exist in reality, and Popper does not deny this. Nonetheless, his critical rationalism does not authorise any logical relation between favourable evidence and the acceptance of a hypothesis, but only its opposite, i.e. falsifying evidence and its rejection (Harré, 1984: 64ff.). In this sense, existential statements, which require some degree of evidence, are excluded from the realm of science. Existential statements, since they cannot be falsified by counter examples, are metaphysical statements which should be sharply differentiated from empirical ones (falsifiable). Once again, we find a certain difficulty in transcending the empiricist tradition which neo-positivists such as Lazarsfeld and Popper criticise, and this generates a particular social ontology.

Methodological nominalism is mutated into *social* nominalism by implicitly assuming that, although both universal laws and singular statements transcend experience, the more abstract the dispositional term involved in a theoretical concept, the more it transcends experience. In this sense, given the need to ground the existence of some of the objects designated by science, Popper seems to assume that individuals are, in some sense, more concrete (or less abstract) than collective entities. According to his nominalist rule, collectivities are not concrete natural entities, but abstract models constructed to interpret certain abstract relations between individuals (Popper, 1957). Society is, thus, nothing more than an aggregate of individuals, and their 'social environment is constituted by "interpersonal relations".' (Archer, 1995: 43). In his own words:

Most of the objects of social science, if not all of them, are abstract objects; they are theoretical constructions. (Even 'the war', or 'the army' are abstract concepts, strange as this may sound to some. What is concrete is the many who are killed, or the men and women in uniform, etc.). These objects, these theoretical constructions used to interpret our experience are the result of constructing certain models (especially of institutions), in order to explain certain experiences.

(Popper, 1957: 135)

For this reason:

The task of social theory is to construct and to analyse our sociological models carefully in descriptive or nominalist terms, that is to say, in terms of individuals, of their attitudes, expectations, etc. – a postulate which may be called methodological individualism.

(ibid.: 136)

Even though Popper is not particularly concerned about the genesis of models, concepts and hypotheses in general, arguing that they do not belong in the realm of methodological considerations, his situational analysis draws on the assumption that, in the social sciences, we already have some intuitive knowledge which can be used to frame hypotheses about people's behaviour. This idea rests on rationalist principles. According to Popper, concrete social situations, i.e. interpersonal relations between individuals, have an element of rationality which allows for the construction of relatively simple models. The model he has in mind when he writes about the social sciences is his situational analysis.

The central element of situational analysis is the principle of rationality, the 'method of logical or rational reconstruction' or, still, 'the zero method'. This is a logical or a priori principle which cannot be empirically falsified, and it states that social agents always act in an adequate or appropriate way in relation to a given situation. Although the principle itself cannot be tested, the situational analysis which is established with its aid is considered to be testable. A theory of human action, like all scientific knowledge, proceeds by conjectures and refutations, and the importance of the principle of rationality for theories of action is that the former is interpreted as an attempt to solve a (sociological) problem:

By a situational analysis I mean a certain kind of tentative or conjectural explanation of some action which appeals to the situation in which the agent finds himself. ... Admittedly, no creative action can ever be fully explained. Nevertheless, we can try, conjecturally, to give an idealized reconstruction of the problem situation in which the agent found himself, and to that extent make the action 'understandable' (or 'rationally understandable'), that is to say, adequate to his situation as he saw it.

(Popper, 1979: 179)

Apart from being in accordance with the hypothetico-deductive model of scientific theory testing, situational analysis sets the limit between individualism and atomism, because, according to Popper (1983), his realist position, which accepts the existence of some general and non-reducible properties of the world, rejects the idea of ultimate explanation. The aim of science is to explain, and what is used as the *explanans* may become an *explanandum* at another stage of knowledge. This means that scientific theories make assertions about structural or relational properties of the world, of structures which are always in need of explanation in terms of more general properties than those which they describe. The regular or law-like behaviour of individual things has to be explained in terms of their structures, i.e. the laws of Nature state 'structural properties of the world'. However, the natural laws which structure the world do not, according to Popper's realism, establish principles of deterministic necessity, but 'they restrict the (logically) possible choice of singular facts' (Popper, 1965: 428). In other words, causal explanation is never deterministic.

When we apply these considerations to the model described in situational analysis it is possible to see that the social situation is always treated as a descriptive structure which does not necessarily bear any real effects on individual actions. This descriptive character of the social structure is in fact one of the central tenets of Boudon's methodological individualism and, together with the idea that all observation is theory laden, it undermines the deterministic basis of empiricist approaches in social science. Nonetheless, there seems to be a fundamental difference between natural and social structures in Popper's work, and it is the latter conception which is retained by Boudon. Given that social structures are equated to interacting individuals, contrary to natural structures, they do not exist in their own right, but only as methodological devices, as a synopsis of interacting individuals. If they do not exist in their own right, they cannot be considered as the bearers of certain causal powers. When it comes to social reality, thus, Popper's realism 'does not require sophisticated realistic assumptions, apart from the reality of individuals' (Stokes, 1998: 91). For this reason, Popper's anti-determinism in the explanation of social phenomena does not spring from a realist conception of causality (based on the assumption that laws do not establish principles of necessity), but from the purely nominal status attributed to social structures on the basis of both his rationalist criteria of theory building and his empiricist criteria of theory testing.

Boudon's situational analysis is also based on the rationality principle, but his critique of Popper's falsification criterion and his consequent exclusion of concept and model formation from methodology brings him closer to Max Weber's sociological rationalism. The link he establishes between Popper and Weber in defining the rationality principle which supports and reinforces methodological individualism can be illustrated here on the basis of his analysis of the *modus tollens*.

The *modus tollens* is an inference rule from scholastic philosophy which constitutes the basis of Popper's falsificationism and, according to Boudon (1980: 170), it takes the following form: '$(T \rightarrow q^*) \wedge \bar{q} \rightarrow \bar{T}$. If from T we deduce q^* and if q^* contradicts observation, then T is false'.[9] Boudon argues, however, that the criterion of refutability based on the *modus tollens* is not the primary condition of scientificity. There are other conditions, such as generality, specificity, distanciation, etc., which also influence the 'strength' of a theory. The process of theory construction which occurs in the social sciences (and, to a certain extent, also in the natural sciences) refers to a much more complex logic than the one described in the *modus tollens*.

According to the *modus tollens*, a theory T is tested provided one can make at least one deduction q^* which expresses the existence of a given state or property in Nature. If the state deduced from T is actually realised, we can draw the conclusion that so far the theory has been shown not to be false. If, instead, q^* fails to correspond to observation q, T can be said to be false. If q^* and q are congruent with each other, all that can be said is that one cannot conclude that T is false, and this is the only conclusion which can be derived from their congruence.

Boudon's critique of the *modus tollens* rests on various elements taken from the practice of scientific activity. First, he assumes that T can take various forms (they can be formal theories based on logical deduction, or analogical ones, for instance). Second, the relation '$\rightarrow$' does not necessarily refer to logical implication, but it can also take the form of a psychological deduction. What Boudon means by psychological deduction is nothing more than his conception of *Verstehen*. It is a sequence of propositions based not on logical deduction, but on our social experience. Consider the example: 'Decisions are most often taken at the level of central administration. Since political figures have greater power, the political function will consequently have greater prestige.' (Boudon, 1980: 175). This is not a true explanation, but a *verstehende* procedure which provides the basis for explanation. Despite not constituting theories, *strictu sensu*, the propositions contained in such analyses are taken to constitute an important framework for social explanation.

In addition, in practice, q is normally not a single proposition but a set of propositions. The number of propositions contained in q is of considerable importance in the choice of a theory, to the extent that, other things being equal, a theory which has a greater number of propositions contained in q will normally be preferred to one which has a lesser number. It is also important to consider the specificity of the propositions, and the 'distance' between the elements of q, i.e. the different domains to which q applies.

Boudon believes that the Popperian interpretation of the *modus tollens* in its most elementary form and the interpretation of q as a single proposition deprives of any meaning the notion of the truth of a theory. Popper's interpretation of the *modus tollens* makes it impossible to define a criterion of truth, since the falsity criterion is immediately applicable (i.e. if this criterion cannot be falsified, then it is metaphysical). Although Boudon basically agrees with Popper that it is never possible to state whether a theory is true, he believes that it is possible to compare theories in terms of a 'subjective probablility' of their being true. This subjective probability depends on a multidimensional variable, which is the structural complexity of q.[10] Even though it is necessary to agree with Popper that there are no general criteria of truth, contrary to him, there are no general criteria of falsity either: although a theory has to be congruent with observed data, the fact that it fails against them does not necessarily mean that it is false. A theory is held to be true or false 'because we have strong reasons of considering it as such, but there are no general criteria of the strength of a system of reasons ... . As to the criteria mobilised to decide that a system of reasons is stronger than another, they are drawn from a huge reservoir and vary from one question to another.' (Boudon, forthcoming).

The quality, validity or truth of a theory is the subjective correlate of, and is subject to, two types of theoretical criticism: an external critique, based on criteria such as falsifiability, structural complexity of the sets of inference [q] which derive from a theory, etc.; and an internal critique, based on the logical context in which the theories appear, i.e. the more or less defined character of the class of facts relating to the theory, experimental, quasi-experimental or non-experimental situation, characteristics of the available data, the coherence of the concepts applied, etc. (Boudon, 1980; Boudon and Bourricaud, 1982: 430).

In a nutshell, Boudon's critique lies in demonstrating that the *modus tollens* 'is nothing but one of the fundamental structures of induction' and, in this sense, it represents an empiricist or externalist criterion of verification which, when taken in isolation, is 'inadequate to account for the *reality* of scientific work or scientific discovery' (Boudon, 1980: 179). His argument rests on the idea that an internal critique of the paradigmatic (a priori and not empirically verifiable) propositions, may lead to more acceptable concepts which, in their turn, may affect the terms of the logical syllogism. This can be generally interpreted as the acceptance of Popper's claims that observation is always theory laden, without relegating 'problems of abstraction and conceptualisation to the dustbin of the "psychology of science" or left to the mysteries of "genius"' (Sayer, 1992: 169).

Boudon's emphasis on rationalist criteria is probably what accounts for some interpretations of his methodological individualism as bearing a closer relation to Weber's interpretive sociology than to Popper's methodological nominalism and its consequent rule of reducing collective to individual properties (see Di Nuoscio, 1996: 33). The importance of Weberian methodology in this respect is that it takes concept formation very seriously.

According to Weber's well-known definition which opens *Economy and Society* (Weber, 1978), sociology 'is a science concerning itself with the interpretive understanding of social action and thereby with a causal explanation of its causes and consequences'. Action is intrinsically linked to meaning, and the apprehension of meaning, understanding, or *Verstehen*, represents a central issue in Weberian methodology. The emphasis on subjective, as opposed to cultural, meaning is guaranteed to the extent that individuals are taken to be the only bearers of meaning.[11] Weber's definition of sociology implies a different justification for methodological individualism (other than reduction based on empiricist criteria), for it rests on the assumption that society cannot exist without individual action. Moreover, it implies that human action is not possible without individuals having some conception of what they are doing and why they are doing things in a certain way.

It is also important to consider that, for Weber, *Verstehen* plays an important role both in the identification of what constitutes the domain of the socio-cultural sciences and in guiding the formation of concepts relative to that domain. This to the extent that a correctly attributed socio-cultural predicate is always an understandable predicate (*Verstehen predicate*) (Oakes, 1977). A socio-cultural predicate is essentially a concept but, contrary to the empiricist epistemology which informed the reductionist naturalism of positivist approaches, social concepts do not consist of a mere description of external (observable) events. This is in fact one of the main tenets of a rationalist epistemology which is central to Weber, Boudon and, to a certain extent, Popper. Referring to the exchange of two objects between a European man and a black African and to the possibility of considering these reciprocally oriented actions as an economic exchange (i.e. as a social relation and a cultural phenomenon), Weber (1977: 109) writes:

> We are inclined to think that a mere description of what can be observed during this exchange – muscular movements and, if some words are 'spoken', the sounds which, so to say, constitute the 'matter' or 'material' behaviour – would in no sense comprehend the 'essence' of what happens. ... The 'essence' of what happens is constituted by the 'meaning' which the two parties ascribe to their observable behaviour, a 'meaning' which 'regulates' the course of their future conduct. Without this 'meaning', we are inclined to say, an exchange is neither empirically possible nor conceptually imaginable.

According to this passage, an adequate apprehension of what is going on cannot rest on observation alone, and, in this sense, the concepts built with the aim of explaining social phenomena cannot rely (solely) on empirical or observable elements. To think otherwise was, according to Boudon (1994), one of Durkheim's most serious mistakes, a mistake which led him to deny the importance of human agency in the explanation of social phenomena in his methodological works.

The distinction between Weber's and Durkheim's positions in this matter is regarded by Boudon as one of the most fundamental in the philosophy of science, and it is expressed by him in terms of an empiricist or externalist epistemology in opposition to a non-empiricist or internalist one. Whereas the former is characterised by the assessment of theories and concepts in terms of Popperian criteria, i.e. mainly by their congruence with (observable) phenomena, the latter does not consider these criteria as being always applicable, always sufficient, or that they are always the most important. The consistency of concepts and theories has to be related to factual and epistemological propositions and, among the latter, the most important are what Boudon calls 'psychological propositions'. They account for what happens in the minds of the agents concerned, making their actions understandable in the same way advocated by the methodology of *Verstehen*.

Given the importance attributed to agents' conceptions in the construction of social reality (which does not mean that their conceptions are necessarily true), both Weber and Boudon claim that, in order for understanding to occur, it is necessary to build concepts which adequately describe the meanings which were present in agents' minds, guiding their behaviour. Weber's answer to this problem appears under the category of 'dogmatics of meaning', i.e. as the attribution of a meaning to the actions of the agents without knowing whether it corresponds to their real meanings, and then questioning how they would have acted in that case in order to compare this ideal reconstruction with what happened in reality. Even though that comparison can be questioned on the grounds that it implies the possibility of direct, immediate access to the reality which is to be compared with the ideal type, the important thing to retain here is that the attribution of certain states, entities and so on cannot be established by deductive reasoning alone (which does not allow for the inclusion of anything but what is already given in the premises of the argument). The building of ideal types, based on neo-Kantian epistemology, rests on the use of a particular kind of inference known as 'abduction', i.e. a process which generates explanatory hypotheses by reference to metaphors and analogies to known or familiar mechanisms (Passmore, 1994; Baert, 1995).

In Weber's dogmatics of meaning, two methodological considerations are required: the rationality of agents and the notion of interaction as regulated by norms. These considerations are, according to Weber (1978: 113), 'heuristic principles to the formulation of hypotheses', and constitute the core of what Boudon (1994) calls the 'psychology of convention', which grounds his psychological propositions. The purpose of the rationality principle is, according to Weber, to access the causal significance of certain actions to a given phenomenon:

> For the purposes of a typological scientific analysis it is convenient to treat all irrational, affectually determined elements of behaviour as factors of deviation from a conceptually pure type of rational action. ... The construction of a purely rational course of action in such cases serves the sociologist as a type (ideal type) which has the merit of clear understandability and lack of ambiguity. By comparison with this it is possible to understand the ways in which actual action is influenced by

irrational factors of all sorts, such as affects and errors, in that they
account for the deviation from the line of conduct which would be
expected on the hypothesis that the action was purely rational.

(Weber, 1978: 6)

The hypotheses established in this way constitute a category which Weber
calls 'objective possibility'. It is called objective possibility to distinguish it
from probability or accidentality and because of the objectivity relating to
the rules of experience, i.e. to the knowledge of the researcher about the
basic progression of the relevant events (Segady, 1987). In this sense,
understanding is not only related to the action itself, but also to the situation
or context in which it happens. There are, thus, two kinds of knowledge
involved in the establishment of 'objective possibility': ontological knowledge,
concerning the facts belonging to the situation in question; and nomological
knowledge, relative to the ways in which people normally act in a given
situation (Weber, 1992).

Although Boudon does not make any direct reference to Weber's category
of objective possibility, he retains its basic idea by means of Popper's
situational analysis. The combination of the Weberian notion of *Verstehen*
and the Popperian situational analysis allows Boudon to construct the neo-
Weberian model of social explanation which summarises his paradigm of
action.

Boudon's conception of nominalist or formal sociology implies that the
formal character of concepts refers to both individual and collective
properties, and this suggests a very indirect relation between nominalism
and social nominalism. However, the problem which arises with the use of
such models is how to guarantee that the sociologist is not closed in an ideal
world created by him or herself and which bears no relation to reality. Boudon
partially resolves this problem with the adoption of the Popperian criterion
of falsification whenever possible:

> [T]he verification of the analysis can be made, and has the advantage of
> being made, on two levels: *at the m level*, that of understanding: we
> shall try, if that is possible, to verify whether the psychological
> mechanisms postulated by the observer, informed of the main data of
> the situation S, correspond to reality. *At the M level*: we shall verify
> whether the consequences at the aggregate level of the microsociological
> hypotheses *m* conform to the aggregate data as they are empirically
> observed.
>
> (Boudon, 1984: 49)[12]

In other words, Boudon tries to transcend a merely empirical level with the
use of models (or ideal types) which are empirically verified. But given that
this empirical verification is not always possible, it is sometimes substituted
or combined with a theoretical or conceptual verification according to the

tenets of rationalism. This allows him to side-step the empiricist framework which guides Lazarsfeld's and Popper's methodological individualism. Of course such a procedure strictly depends on the quality of the theory informing the research and the verification process, and whether the theory can be considered as anything other than an arbitrary construction. Even though this problem can also be found in Weber's notion of ideal types, I shall deal with problems related to the adequacy of concepts and of theory 'verification' in Chapters 2 and 4 respectively. For now, it is sufficient to show that, according to Boudon's interpretation of the Weber–Popper postulate, methodological individualism, being an anti-empiricist and an anti-essentialist approach, is taken to represent an alternative to both atomism and holism or collectivism.

This alternative to atomism and holism leads to a particular conception of the social actor. Boudon's social actor constitutes a synthesis which tries to go beyond *Homo sociologicus* and *Homo economicus*. Its main characteristics are:

1   The fact that it is established a priori (in the neo-Kantian sense of the term, i.e. it is taken to be a heuristic resource, and not a concrete type or something held to be necessarily true).
2   It is subject to socialisation effects.
3   It has a limited or contextual rationality (later defined in terms of a 'cognitive rationality').
4   Its actions can be regarded as presenting a function of adaptation to a given situation.

This definition of the social actor provides the synthesis of the main positions investigated in this section and is meant to establish a connection between the micro- and macro-levels of social reality, both in the sense that social phenomena have to be explained as the aggregation of individual actions, and that macro phenomena constitute a kind of social *milieu* of the actor. This problem is best conceptualised in terms of the agency–structure debate, which I shall now use to further delineate Boudon's paradigm of action.

Structure, agency and methodological individualism

The structure–agency debate focuses on two fundamental questions for sociological thinking: the problem of how human activity shapes the social world and the question of how the social world moulds human activity (Layder, 1994). Although the debate is sometimes believed to rest on a dualism whose terms are stated as being totally incommensurable and heterogeneous, this view only makes sense in conflationary frameworks that have been set up in terms of a radical holism or a radical individualism.

The first of these frameworks can be illustrated by authors such as

Althusser, through what Susan James calls 'absolute holism' or, in Boudon's terminology, 'totalitarian realism', i.e. the 'attempt to explain *all* social phenomena in terms of certain aspects of social structure, at the expense of explanations which appeal to the properties of individual subjects' (James, 1984: 108). The second framework can be exemplified by the methodological individualism of J. Watkins, a radical version of individualism according to which even ideal-type concepts which are constructed in holistic terms are rendered impossible: 'holistic ideal types, which would abstract essential traits from a social whole while ignoring individuals are impossible: they always turn into individualistic ideal types' (Watkins, 1952: 42).

Both the collectivist and the individualistic views have proved to be problematic. On the one hand, Althusser's notion of history as a process without subjects cannot properly account for social change, for change implies some sort of discontinuity with established social practices, which, in its turn, implies an anthropological dimension of essential human traits. On the other hand, Watkins's argument on the impossibility of coherent holistic concepts points to a serious methodological limitation within his own framework, to the extent that collective ideal types are always presupposed in the explanation of actors' beliefs and dispositions. This limitation is tentatively solved with the idea that, because we cannot regress *ad infinitum* in the explanation process, collective concepts can be used as long as they can be translated into individual types. But, as Maurice Mandelbaum (1992) has shown, the translation of collective ideal types into individual ones implies an equivalence relation between social and individual terms and, in this sense, nothing would prevent sociologists from establishing these relations in holistic terms either.

The debate between individualists and holists took place mainly in the 1950s and, since then, much has been conceded by both sides. In the 1980s, the debate assumed a different form, and sociology experienced a 'movement away from the agency–structure extremism' (Schuurmann, 1994: 25). This movement attempted to integrate different levels of reality, both in the form of the micro–macro debate in North America, and of structure and agency in Europe. In these attempts, micro–macro, structure and agency, individual and society, etc., are viewed in the light of a continuum, but it is not uncommon that different authors tend to favour one or the other extreme of this continuum. The social sciences are still largely represented by reductionist and conflationary views according to which one level of reality is treated as a mere epiphenomenon of the other (Archer, 1995).

Despite the less radical character of this new phase of the structure–agency debate, there are still important differences between sociological theories, and these can be expressed in Derek Layder's (1994: 118) idea that 'the real differences between sociologists arise over the question of *how* human social activities (including the solo activities of individuals) are related to the social contexts in which they are embedded'. It is this relation between human action and the social context in Boudon's work that we shall examine here, and it should be considered that the development of his own work has, to a certain extent, reflected the more general changes within the agency–structure debate which happened between the 1950s and the 1980s.

It is important to notice that Boudon has never actively taken part in the agency–structure debate, but I intend to show here that it is not only possible but also important to see his work from this perspective. First, Boudon's adoption of methodological individualism can be largely regarded as a specific response to the French 'structuralist' production from the 1950s to the 1970s, and it is mainly in terms of this response that one can infer his position in the debate. Second, although his methodological individualism prescribes that social phenomena should be explained on the basis of individual actions, it does not assume that these actions happen in a social vacuum, but they are socially indexed. It is this kind of concern which allows us to place the agency–structure debate at the centre of his approach, albeit in an indirect way. More direct references to the debate can be occasionally found in his work, such as in his formalisation of the neo-Weberian action paradigm and in his analysis of Simmel's philosophy of history (Boudon, 1986b).

This analysis highlights the fact that 'Simmel's basic point is that everything of historical interest is the expression or the product of mental phenomena.' (ibid.: 861). Social phenomena are viewed by Simmel as the result of individuals' actions, which are, in their turn, a product of these individuals' mental processes. Mental processes depend both on historical circumstances and on the situation or social environment in which the actors are, and this is where we can find the explicit link between agency and structure: first, the structural elements of the situation represent external and objective facts which are imposed on the agents, becoming the causes of their mental activity; second, mental activities and actions constitute and transform the social structures (or, in Simmel's language, social forms). In this sense, there is an intrinsic relation between agency and structure to the extent that 'although social phenomena are always the product of individual actions, the actions are part of a context which has a structure: structures can only be understood on the basis of actions and actions can only be understood on the basis of structures' (ibid.: 862).

One question immediately arises from this: Given the anti-realist perspective generally associated with individualism, how can Boudon sustain the link between structure and agency? One of the arguments for individualism seems to focus on what Boudon calls 'totalitarian realism', which is often interpreted in terms of the idea that systems or structures are real and able to produce real effects:

> If it is not realised that any social or historical phenomenon, however immense and complex, can be nothing other than the result of a combination of actions, and consequently, of mental states, one runs

the risk of taking for real something that is but a purely intellectual construct, of lending a causal efficiency to 'forces' that exist only in the mind of the observer.

(Boudon, 1986b: 863)

Structures and collective concepts alike are analytical constructs and, as such, are analytically reducible to the actions of individual actors (Cohn, 1993). However, as I tried to show with his conception of social nominalism, it is not certain that Boudon establishes such a direct link between the non-realist character of social concepts and their reduction to individual ones, at least not throughout his work. Since the concept of individual is also an analytical construct (Boudon, 1996c), there has to be some kind of validating procedure which guarantees the adequacy of sociological concepts, both at the agency and at the structural level. This procedure rests on the internal (rational) and external (empirical) validating criteria of theory testing, but as it was shown with Weber's definition of sociology, the kind of rationalism favoured by Boudon presents a kind of elective affinity with nominalism/ individualism since it equates understanding with retrieving individual mental contents. Given this, it is important to see how Boudon conceives the concept of structure and how it relates to his idea of internal criteria of theory building.

The concept of structure and its relation to theoretical structures

Boudon's definition of structure derives from the analysis of the roles played by the concept of structure in different contexts. This definition corresponds strictly to his and Lazarsfeld's nominalist methodology, according to which the specification of individual (in the sense of isolated) concepts is relatively unimportant: 'what counts are the theoretical structures in which these concepts are combined' (Outhwaite, 1983: 3).

According to Boudon (1968), it is impossible to give an inductive definition to the concept of structure, in the sense of comparing and abstracting the elements common to the object designated by the concept. This is because social structures are not directly observable. The concept of structure is, moreover, a polysemic notion, i.e. it has different meanings. Its polysemic nature can be observed in its synonymic and homonymic associations, both in everyday and in scientific language. As an example of its synonymic associations, it is possible to observe that the concept considered is synonymous with notions like 'system of relationships', 'sum of elements being greater than its parts', 'coherence', etc. Alternatively, it involves certain negative or homonymic associations, such as structure–external associations, structure–aggregate, structure–organisation, etc. In other cases, it cannot be reducible to any of these associations, and the concept assumes different meanings according to the kind of theory to which it is linked. All these differences are functions of the context in which the concept appears, and it is only the analysis of these contexts which provides the meaning of 'structure'.

It is then maintained that, despite the different definitions given to the concept, it has an indisputable identity generated by a transformation in scientific vocabulary, i.e. by the strength of the theories which have been developed with the purpose of explaining particular structures. This identity is, to borrow Popper's expression, a function of the degree of verisimilitude of the theories which account for the concept. This essentially means that, although the concept has not been defined in an uneqivocal way, some of the theories which account for the structural character of an object have a well-defined relation with the (structural) phenomenon they describe, i.e they can be considered as true. In particular, given that Boudon's notion of theory is defined in terms of a hypothetico-deductive system of (generalised) propositions, and that interactionist theories are viewed as the best candidates for filling this role, in his works, structure will be defined in strict conformity to an interactionist paradigm of social action.

Boudon identifies two main contexts where this concept appears: definitional and operative contexts. In the first type of context, 'structure' is used either to emphasise the systemic nature of an object, i.e. to indicate that one is dealing with interdependent variables, or to stress that a certain method is applied in the description of an object as a system (Boudon, 1968: 35). In operative contexts, the concept of structure is incorporated within a theory which attempts to account for the systematic nature of an object (which obviously implies that a certain meaning is attached to the term, but not as the main aim of the theory). The difference between them is also described by Boudon as a search for a meaning for the concept of structure, in definitional or intentional contexts, and an attempt to determine the structure of a given object, in operative ones.

The roles played by each of these contexts vary enormously, and they are analysed through a series of examples extracted from psychology, sociology, anthropology and linguistics. Starting from intentional definitions, Boudon states that most frequently the term structure appears in opposition to other terms, and in such a way that the former could be replaced by any other equivalent term without losing its meaning. In other instances, the concept is opposed to terms like organisation or conjuncture, and its role is basically the same as in the preceding case: it indicates that we oppose certain categories of objects, or certain ways of apprehending them, in a way that one of the terms in the opposition relates to the synonymic associations of the term structure.

When the concept appears in this type of context without being opposed to other terms, most of the time it serves only to point out that the object is viewed as a system or a whole which must be grasped if the behaviour of its parts is to be understood. For this reason, it is not possible to account for a single definition of 'structure' in this kind of context; any attempt to express the content of this term is bound be reduced to the enumeration of the associations and oppositions evoked because the concept of structure has no other content than that. It is thus defined by associations such as structure–totality, structure–systems of relationships, structure–whole irreducible to the sum of its parts, structure–essence, etc.; as well as by the oppositions structure–outward appearance, structure–observable characteristics, structure–aggregate, structure–superficial system, etc. (ibid.: 79). The identity of the concept of structure in intentional definitional contexts is thus related to this kind of constitutional definition, and, in accordance with the best nominalist tradition, only in this sense has it an identity and a single meaning.

The second type of context is said to represent a development of the first, in the sense that the duality of contexts represents two different stages in the analysis of a given subject. This idea is intimately related to Boudon's conception of theory, in the strictest sense in which he conceives the term, roughly, as a hypothetico-deductive system of ('well-established') propositions. The passage from the first to the second type of context is, according to Boudon, an attempt to construct scientific theories which follows from the realisation that the subject matter presents regularities, that its elements are interdependent, in other words, that it has a 'structure'.

It is in the light of this continuum between definitional and operative contexts that Boudon justifies the term 'intentional definitions' in definitional contexts: it represents the intention to construct or to develop a theory by analysing the interdependence of the elements of an object-system. However, Boudon points out, it is very common that such an intent does not lead to an operative implementation or that such an implementation is rendered impossible, either because the object itself does not allow it, or because the necessary mental tools are not available.

The concept of structure in operative contexts is thus associated with a logical construct (a hypothetico-deductive theory) which, when applied to a given object-system, defines the structure of this object. In this way, the concept of structure, and the correlate adjective 'structural', has a homonymic character in the operational context, i.e. the same term has different meanings according to the theory to which it is attached. According to Boudon, there are two sources of homonymy: the first is related to the level of testability of a hypothetico-deductive theory (testable, indirectly testable or untestable). The second is related to the object itself, that is, to the way in which it is conceived and bound to be observed or inferred. Given his anti-essentialism, for Boudon, the structural qualities of an object are not intrinsic to the object in the sense that they represent its 'essence'. What is at stake is not the notion of essence, but that of sense or meaning, and meaning is, according to him, strictly linked to the theory in which the term appears. Nonetheless, a structural analysis should, according to him, also refer *to the object's properties* and, in this sense, it generates a coherent account of facts which, on the phenomenological level, appear as incoherent.

In analysing different types of theories, according to their testable or non-testable character and to the types of objects that they deal with, Boudon concludes that the structural analyses undertaken by various authors are always related to axioms from which the interdependence between elements of a system or the impossibility of certain combinations of elements is deduced (Boudon, 1968: 185). At the same time, he insists that the structure of an object can only be outlined by a theory, and one can only speak of a structural method if by this is meant a 'very general "perspective" which consists in conceiving the object to be analysed as a whole, as a set of interdependent elements whose coherence has to be demonstrated' (ibid.: 213).[13] What is not acceptable for him is the idea of a structural method in the sense of a set of methodological rules for the construction of theories; a 'structural method' is not really a method, but a class of theories whose specific character consists in attempting to account for the systematic nature of the objects with which they deal. The quality of these theories will, according to him, depend on the imagination of its authors in postulating certain (non-observable) properties or states, on previous research and on the characteristics of the objects studied. Of course, the imagination element is seriously affected within a deductive conception of theory since deductive models of explanation do not allow for the inclusion of anything but what is already given in the premises of the argument (or the theory), and this, together with the idealistic character of ideal-type models, represents an element of scepticism in relation to the use of structural models. As it will become clear later, this does not have the same deleterious effect on the agency level insofar as its models are based on 'psychological deduction', i.e. on the deduction from elements which are, more often than not, outside a given theoretical structure, thus allowing for the use of a non-empiricist epistemology by means of abductive (or retroductive) arguments.

Since the notion of structure is so closely related to the notion of theory, it is probably clear by now that the stronger the theory, the more coherent and systematic the structure which is revealed. It is necessary, thus, to make a brief reference to Boudon's definition of theory. The importance of this is that, contrary to models or ideal types, for Boudon, theories can be used as truth-functional definitions of reality, and not only as models which have no strict relations with it.

Like the notion of structure, the notion of theory in the social sciences is a polysemic one, this time due to the failure to always distinguish between theories, in the strict sense, and paradigms. In the narrow sense, theory corresponds to the notion of a hypothetico-deductive system of propositions, whereas a paradigm corresponds to the idea that it is possible to extract propositions from a set of primary propositions by analogy or subsumption, but not by deduction. In the broad sense, however, the notion of theory includes at least three distinct categories of paradigms classified by Boudon as theoretical or analogical, formal and conceptual. Theoretical or analogical paradigms are characterised by the fact that the *explanans* is drawn by analogy from a body of knowledge belonging to another domain. Formal and conceptual paradigms, in their turn, 'constitute frameworks of reference which provide explanatory propositions with either the elements of conceptual systems (conceptual paradigms) or syntactic rules (formal paradigms)' (Boudon, 1980: 156).

Formal and conceptual paradigms work as the functional equivalents of theories in the narrow sense because they give rise to generalisation and explanation. This functional equivalence is intimately related to the fact that 'the logical situations which these disciplines [the social sciences] encounter whenever they seek to explain this or that social phenomenon, are diverse and cannot always be reduced to epistemological models sprung from the natural sciences and the physico-chemical sciences in particular' (ibid.: 167). Scientific progress, especially in the social sciences, often takes the form of generalisation of a paradigm, or of the transmutation of an analogical into a formal paradigm, of a conceptual paradigm into a formal one or of the introduction of new paradigms and the criticism of existing ones. In theory, this should apply to any level of research, but it is not difficult to perceive that, according to the interactionist rule of conceiving structures as the aggregation of actions, social structures do not present any particular or emergent properties which are intrinsic to them, thus allowing us to treat them as really existing things.

Concluding remarks

The aim of this chapter consisted in locating Boudon's thought within some general traditions, showing, at the same time, its specificity. Sharing a common concern with other French authors of his generation, he maintained a strong opposition to the deterministic and reductionist claims of structuralism. Contrary to those authors, Boudon identified himself with a nominalist or individualist tradition according to which social phenomena have to be explained by recourse to the actions and mental contents of socially situated individuals.

By combining Popper's situational analysis and Weber's notion of *Verstehen*, Boudon developed a paradigm of social action which is taken to rest on two main principles: methodological individualism and a rationality principle. Methodological individualism is generally associated with a (methodological) nominalism which intends to oppose empirical realism's claims that theoretical concepts have to be based on the observation of atomistic objects and events. This accounts for the use of models or ideal types in the explanation, and the theories built with their aid have to be judged against both external or empirical criteria and internal or rationalist ones.

The use of formal models would allow for the use of metaphors, such as social structure, which would provide the context in which actions happen. However, given the unavoidable links between theory, methodology and ontology, it is possible to observe an implicit social ontology which springs from the heuristic character which is attributed to the notion of structure and other collective concepts. This is largely due to Boudon's refusal to consider theoretical descriptions of social structures as truth-functional descriptions of emergent and non-reducible properties based on non-empirical criteria of theory testing. But given its central role in the explanation of action, it remains to be seen whether Boudon is able to maintain this position in his substantive analyses.

2 Linking structure and agency in Boudon's substantive analyses

As I have tried to show in the preceding chapter, interactionist paradigms vary according to the research problem and, consequently, to the types of elements which need to be taken into account in the explanation of a particular social phenomenon. Given that the neo-Weberian paradigm synthesises the main positions of the interactionist family, the different phenomena with which Boudon deals throughout his work provide different relations between agency and structure.

In order to investigate the links between agency and structure in Boudon's substantive analyses, I will classify his work according to different phases.[1] The first of these phases, which I shall call zero phase, refers to his quest to develop a mathematical language for the social sciences. Its main representative is a book based on his doctoral thesis, *L'Analyse Mathématique des Faits Sociaux*. Insofar as his concern with mathematical formalisation was merely transitory and does not occur in the rest of his work, I deliberately exclude it from this book.

The second phase, which I take to be the early development of his current ideas, is represented here by his works on the sociology of education, developed in the early 1970s. Here one can see the seeds of an individualistic approach, which is further elaborated in his reflections on the unintended consequences of social action (or perverse effects). This is followed by a return to the notion of social system in *La Logique du Social* (1979), when the tension regarding an individualistic analysis which tries to take into account the external and objective character of social structures becomes more explicit. This movement constitutes what I call 'the intermediate phase', and the methodological position adopted here can be considered as more or less definitive.

The most recent phase, from the mid-1980s onwards, does not present any substantial methodological shifts since *La Logique du Social*, but is characterised instead by thematic and stylistic ones: the thematic unit became the study of ideas, and the style becomes more and more essaystic. Nonetheless, these thematic and stylistic changes do not come for free. Despite the fact that there are no substantial changes in terms of methodology, it is possible to observe the development of a less utilitarian approach. In fact, the more Boudon moves towards ideas whose objectivity is difficult to establish, the less utilitarian-oriented he becomes, giving rise to a much more complex notion of rationality and generating a more socially and culturally grounded conception of human agent.

The early phase: the sociology of education

Boudon's early phase is characterised by the study of structural or macro-social variables and their relations and, despite his early affinities with Lazarsfeld's nominalism, it is in his book *Education, Opportunity and Social Inequality* (1974) that his theoretical models start to gain an individualistic gloss (in the sense of methodological individualism). I believe it is not inaccurate to say that this was the work which made Boudon known world-wide, presenting him with the Girardeau Prize from the Académie des Sciences Morales et Politiques. *Education, Opportunity and Social Inequality* was published for the first time in France in 1973, and the third edition was published in 1985. It has been translated into English, Italian, Portuguese, Spanish and Japanese, and, almost 30 years after its publication, the theory developed there continues to inspire many contemporary works, such as the work of Volker Mueller-Benedictin in Germany, Gudmund Hernes in Norway and Nathalie Bulle in France.

The book deals with two sociological problems: the inequality of educational opportunities and social mobility. Inequality of educational opportunity (IEO) is described as the differences in the level of *educational attainment* according to social background. Social mobility (or immobility) is defined as differences in *social achievement* according to social background. In this restricted sense, social mobility can also be called inequality of social opportunity (ISO). The amount of educational inequality can be considered as the probabilities associated with educational attainment as a function of social background; for instance, a society in which the probability of going to college is lower for a worker's than for a lawyer's child is characterised by a certain amount of IEO. Likewise, a society is characterised by a certain amount of ISO if the probability of reaching a high social status is lower for the former child.

At the time the book was written, the relation between education and social mobility was based on the assumption that the main function of school was to select individuals so as to guarantee as strict as possible a relation between their capacities and the capacities required by the various jobs and positions which characterise the socio-professional structure. From this assumption, it was deduced that the inequality of educational opportunities is largely responsible for the intensity of social and professional immobility from one generation to the other. As a corollary, it was generally accepted that a decrease in the inequality of educational opportunities would be followed by a decrease in social immobility between generations (Boudon, 1981).

The empirical falsity of the argument was, nonetheless, demonstrated through the following paradoxes:

1   In spite of a slow but inexorable decrease in inequality of educational opportunities in recent decades (the book was written in the early 1970s), there has been only a modest effect on social mobility to the extent that demotion or ascent from one generation to the other has occurred to a much smaller extent than formerly.
2   Although some countries, such as the United States, Sweden, Norway and the United Kingdom, presented a much lower inequality of educational opportunities than others, e.g. Germany, France and Switzerland, statistical data from the 1960s to the 1970s show that social immobility was no less pronounced in the first set of countries.
3   According to the same propositions, a decrease in the inequality of educational opportunities should lead to a reduction in income inequalities, but this also did not agree with the empirical data gathered by Boudon.

Boudon argues that the paradoxes described above result from an inadequacy of the instruments of statistical and theoretical analysis normally employed and, in order to solve the problem raised by the establishment of a direct causal relation between inequality of educational opportunities, social mobility and income inequalities, he suggests a model based on systems analysis. This means that social inequalities (including social mobility) must be considered as the result of a complex set of determinants whose influences cannot be taken in isolation, but must be considered as a system. The expectation of a mechanistic relation between the different forms of inequality is then replaced by a probabilistic approach in which the relations between two (or more) variables are viewed as the consequence of an intricate set of structural factors.

Before I proceed to describe the model developed in this book, I would like to emphasise that I will be going in the opposite direction to Boudon's. Whereas his purposes are substantive rather than methodological, I am concerned here with the latter.[2] In this sense, I will attempt to show the methodological implications of the model without worrying much about its substantive content. It should also be considered that the methodological consequences in which I am interested here refer mainly to the problem of how Boudon relates structure and agency. Since this problem is perfectly well illustrated in the IEO model, I will not refer to the construction of an ISO model and the relations between IEO and ISO.

The construction of an IEO model starts with the analysis of data showing the link between the level of educational attainment and mobility. Based on these data, Boudon argues that, in spite of the general assumption that industrial societies are largely meritocratic, there does not seem to exist a high correlation between educational level and social status: there is a low correlation between a son's educational level relative to his father's and a son's relative status, and also a low correlation between a son's absolute educational level and his social status relative to his father's (Boudon, 1974: 11).

He then proceeds to show that the social status that individuals achieve is the result of a two-stage filtering process: 'In the first stage they go from a given social background to a given educational level. In the second stage they go from education level to achieved status. In both cases, the filtering process has been assumed to be inequalitarian.' (ibid.: 21). In this process, both the educational and social structures are considered as given, or as determined by exogenous factors. Nevertheless, Boudon argues that this is realistic only insofar as the social structure is concerned; for example, although someone might have the aptitude to fill a certain type of job and to achieve the social status related to that job, this job must first exist. On the other hand, the educational structure, or rather, the educational distribution, is in most cases an effect of individual will to the extent that an individual cannot create a position in the professional market, but he/she can go to university provided he/she is qualified.

Boudon's analysis of educational distribution goes against two main theories dealing with IEO: the first one is what he calls the 'value theory', according to which 'the main factor responsible for IEO is the existence of different values among the various social classes'; that is, 'people's evaluation of what social achievement means and of what might be considered efficient routes towards achieving it vary as a function of their social backgrounds. Consequently, people of different social classes attach different values to education.' (ibid.: 22). The second is represented by the 'culture theory', which posits that IEO is mainly generated by 'the differences in cultural opportunities afforded by their families according to their social background' (ibid.: 23), or, in other words, by the distance between what is positively valued and taught at school, on the one hand, and at home, on the other. Both theories present serious limitations in dealing with reality: the value theory tends to overlook the numerous deviant cases relating to class values; the cultural theory, in its turn, limits the effects of stratification to cultural differences, leaving aside other sources of IEO, which would characterise it as a hyperculturalist approach. Reacting against both determinism and causal mononism, Boudon proposes the development of what he terms 'the social position theory'.

According to the social position theory, there is no need to assume that different social classes attach different values to education, only that the expectations of individuals must be related to their origins. In this sense, if both lower-class and middle-class individuals want to become lawyers, their level of aspiration is not the same; the former's is higher, since he or she has to travel a greater distance to achieve it. This means that the costs and benefits associated with a given educational level or with a given status differ according to social background.

The importance of this theoretical scheme is that it provides not only the explanation of the primary effects of stratification, that is, cultural inequalities, but also the deviation from the expected norms of class culture. This deviation is shown to be a function of (individual) properties such as IQ, school achievement, verbal achievement, etc., which tend to compensate the cultural differences related to social class, thus assuming a very important role for lower-class students. Regarding the problem that interests me here, the model shows an intrinsic link between structure and agency: although both educational and status aspirations vary within a particular social class as an effect of those individual properties, the initial cultural differences between social classes do have an effect on those aspirations, which tend to be greater, the lower the social class.

In this way, the model accounts for both primary effects of the stratification system (cultural inequalities) and secondary effects of the stratification system (which Boudon defines as expectations and aspirations which are not mediated by cultural inequality, but by individual properties such as IQ, school achievement, etc). In other words, what the model introduces is the assumption that the importance attached to educational choices relates to the social status of the individual, and that this is an important effect which is not accounted for in cultural theories. IEO is thus generated by a two-component process: one is related to the cultural effects of the stratification system, and the other component is based on the assumption that, *ceteris paribus*, people make their choices according to their position in the stratification system or the parameters of their decisional fields are a function of their position in the stratification system.

The introduction of an 'individualistic approach' in the analysis of the educational structure seems to have at least one direct implication for the structure–agency problem: that there is no direct and mechanical relation between the social structure in general and the educational structure, since the latter depends on individual *choices* and these choices are not *determined* by the social structure. The model thus entails a probabilistic analysis which involves a two-stage mechanism:

1   A sample of students is chosen in order to form a school cohort which is then broken down into sub-samples which are functions of family background. These sub-samples are then distributed in a Cartesian space where the students with 'lower' social background are more likely to be located in the less favourable corner of the space, and vice versa. The differences in the distribution are then a function of family background on intermediate variables (such as family cultural endowments, attitudes, interests, etc.).

2   For each type of social background a curve is drawn in the Cartesian space, and each has a certain probability (this probability can refer to surviving school beyond a certain point, for instance, or to choosing a general, rather than a vocational, course). The result is that the

probability *p* will be higher, the closer the curve is to the most favourable corner of the Cartesian space, i.e. *p* is likely to be higher, the higher the social background.

(Boudon, 1974: 67)

This makes it possible to statistically predict the educational future of a hypothetical group of students. Nevertheless, this representation only reproduces the data provided by cross-sectional surveys, i.e. it is a static picture of IEO. Boudon's concerns turn then into how to transform this scheme into a model that is dynamic in relation to individuals and to the school system. The system-dynamic model takes into account the following axioms:

1   The distribution of students in the Cartesian space is a function of social background.
2   The values which characterise any individual on any dimension (age, school achievement, etc.) of the Cartesian space are not subject to change over time. This assumption relative to age means that his/her relative age in relation to his/her peers (old or young) will remain constant at each school grade.
3   A school system can be represented as a sequence of *x* branching points, each describing an alternative like, say, stay in or leave a higher curriculum (HC).
4   Given a particular school system, at each of the *x* branching points a set of probabilities is defined. *Ceteris paribus*, the probabilities are higher, the higher the social background. In the same way, the more favourable the position of an individual on any dimension of the Cartesian space, the higher the probability associated with it.
5   'Because of the effect of certain exogenous variables (for instance, an overall increase in living standards), the probabilities of staying in HC in a given school system at any grade increase over time' (ibid.: 71). But this increase is subject to a ceiling effect, i.e. 'a probability that is already high will increase less than a low probability in the same time period' (ibid.: 76). This happens because, when a social class sends 10% of its potential students to university in a given period of time, this percentage may double in the following period, but this is logically impossible when the initial percentage corresponds to, say, 90%. This last axiom is actually what gives the dynamic aspect of the model.

When this model is operationalised, it is possible to determine the alteration, in time, in the composition of social classes relative to each educational level. The results from this dynamic model differ from the ones attained in cross-sectional analyses, where both primary and secondary effects of stratification are equally important. According to the results obtained, it is possible to conclude that, even when the effects of cultural inequality have been eliminated, the rates of disparity between lower- and higher-class students attending college remain very high, albeit reduced. In this sense, over time and other things being equal, secondary effects of stratification play a much more important role in the rates of disparity in question. As a corollary, 'the attendance at college of a disproportionate number of students from the higher class is probably much more attributable to the different *systems of expectations* generated by different social backgrounds than to the different cultural backgrounds that are due to the same source' (ibid.: 85).

The explanation of the observed tendencies can be summarised in the following argument: in the first place, lower-class youngsters tend to be culturally disadvantaged and hence to be low achievers at school. But this tendency is not always followed. If the student is relatively bright, he or she is likely to survive beyond a branching point, with probabilities which may be as high as that of a higher-class student. This means that, after a number of years, differences in school achievement as a direct result of the social background are scarcely observed in a cohort of students. In other words, after some time, the effect of cultural differences (or primary effects of stratification) dies out. Secondary effects of stratification, on the other hand, not only do not die out, but they increase over time. Differences in expectation and aspiration as a function of social stratification (secondary effects of stratification) exist throughout time, regardless of the school level at which the observation is made.

What are, for Boudon, the methodological consequences of this model? According to him, the model tells us that the connection between social class and educational achievement, or between social stratification and educational distribution, can only be understood if they are considered as the aggregation of individual choices; thus, there is no reason for an absolute correlation between two structural variables, which have to be mediated by the notion of action (Boudon and Bourricaud, 1982).

The point I want to concentrate on now is the role of action in this mediation. The analysis actually rests on a sequence of the type: low status → low school achievement → lack of enthusiasm for higher education → low attendance at higher levels of education. This is, roughly speaking, the structural aspect of the analysis, insofar as it shows structural tendencies. But this aspect is then combined with elements belonging to the action framework which account for the reflexive character of human agency based on the existence of certain individual properties. It is in fact the 'creative' aspects of human agency that allow Boudon to break with structural determinism without altogether disregarding the social structure's effects. This is done by introducing intermediate concepts which link structure and agency, such as the different dimensions of 'social position' (social class, cultural endowments, etc.). These dimensions actually represent a point of contact between social and individual properties, and when there is not a causal effect of certain individual properties (IQ, verbal achievement, etc.)

which can change the direction of the sequence above, individuals will indeed be 'directed' by external factors. Moreover, the fact that at least some individual attributes are a function of their social position is not excluded, nor that the social structure directs (or qualifies) the actors' expectations and aspirations.

It is interesting to notice that Boudon (1982) argues that there is some sort of structural determinism in his model of education, but he insists on the fact that the kind of determinism involved is fundamentally different from what he calls 'determinist paradigms'. His model, or paradigm, constitutes a 'methodological determinism', i.e. 'a paradigm in which the only propositions used are those that both obey a determinist syntax (propositions of the type "A (prior to B) *explains* B") and yet remain compatible with interactionist interpretation' (ibid.: 197). This is indeed a sound conclusion; what does not sound accurate is his argument that the difference between the two types of determinism lies in the *realist* character of the interpretation of the relations observed. According to him, if the statistical relation is interpreted in realist terms, one will have a hyperculturalist, hyperfunctionalist or totalitarian realist paradigm. If, on the other hand, the relation is taken as a 'synopsis of actions' whose logical structure has to be understood at a later stage, the model is determinist only at the methodological level: 'In the latter situation I will take the statistical relation to be a descriptive fact that needs explaining and I will construct a generative model of the interactionist type to make such an explanation feasible' (ibid.: 198). A causal relation (of the kind P→P′) is thus taken to be a descriptive proposition which has to be explained at the level of actions and, therefore, considered as an effect of composition.

I would argue that to emphasise the descriptive or non-realist character of structural relations does not help to explain social action. In fact, it is evident that, without recourse to elements such as class norms, Boudon will never be able to explain certain types of action. This is not because of the impossibility of a *regressio ad infinitum*, but because, as he himself recognised (Boudon, 1974), individual will is not dissociated from social factors.

Contrary to Boudon's arguments, there is no need for individualism in order to conceive of causal relations in a non-deterministic way. And, I believe that Boudon's model of education does not necessarily entail that conclusion. The link between structure and agency does not have to be understood in terms of deterministic relations (whether at an ontological or at a methodological level), but a possible alternative to both sociologism and individualism is to interpret the link between agency and structure in terms of a critical realist perspective which is implicitly, if incompletely, developed by Boudon.

It has already been argued that Boudon's anti-realism is generally opposed to essentialism, and that the latter position can, to a certain extent, be associated with a particular ontology generated by empirical realism. Contrary to that view, critical realists argue that reality cannot be conceived as constituted by atomistic phenomena and events, but as being structured and stratified. In other words, reality includes not only what can be accessed by direct observation (the empirical domain), but also what Bhaskar (1997) has called the domains of the *actual* (experiences and events which may or may not be observed) and the *real* (the processes or structures which generate events). The existence of an actual domain implies that experience does not exhaust reality, for something may happen without its being observed. The existence of a real domain, in its turn, implies that events do not account for everything that happens in reality either, for some processes or mechanisms may be blocked by other mechanisms, thus leading to no particular event.

According to this approach, the explanation should be based on a conception of causal law that is relative to mechanisms which, in their turn, refer to the modes of behaviour of entities, expressing their tendencies, dispositions, liabilities, forms of action or causal powers. This means that, contrary to the Humean conception of law shared by positivists, causal laws are intrinsically related to the objects or agents to which they refer, and should not be mistaken for something generated by the human mind, such as heuristic devices or, in Hume's language, 'psychological necessities'.

According to this conception of causal law, the explanatory model developed by realists introduces the notion of agency in the causal story, a notion which accounts for specific ways of acting of objects, for their nature and causal powers. According to Harré (1986: 284), for instance, the structure of a causal explanation of an observable phenomenon takes the following form: 'A *Particular Being* has a *Tendency* which if *Released*, in a certain type of situation, is manifested in some observable *Action* but when *Blocked* has no observable effect'. The notion of agency implicit in this model refers to causal powers which may or may not be actualised, because, in the real world, which is an open or non-experimental system, mechanisms operate alongside other mechanisms which co-determine the event or phenomenon in question. In this sense, the absence of an event does not necessarily signify that there are no underlying tendencies at work, but it may mean that they are being neutralised by other tendencies (countervailing tendencies) and, for this reason, do not actualise. Even though these tendencies or causal powers may not actualise, they are considered to be (at least potentially) operative, defining the nature or properties of the object or agent in question. Therefore, 'the relation between what a thing is and what it is capable of doing and undergoing is naturally necessary' (Harré and Madden, 1998: 109), and the notion of natural necessity implies that causal powers and relations are intrinsically related: causes do have the power to generate their effects and there is a real (material, not only logical) relation between these things, even though this relation is normally beyond what we can experience (Halfpenny, 1994).

The idea that the tendencies or causal powers of an object define the nature of this object does not imply essentialism, for this nature does not refer to fixed and immutable essences. Scientific concepts are never 'finished' or true in an a priori sense, but are always subject to modification: whenever a new tendency is identified, it should be incorporated into the concept in question, modifying it. There is thus a two-way relation between conceptual activity and empirical investigation, characterising scientific activity as a 'process-in motion' whose dialectics has not a foreseeable end: 'In science, there is a kind of dialectic in which a regularity is identified, a plausible explanation for it is invented, and the reality of the entities and process postulated in the explanation is then checked' (Bhaskar, 1997: 14).

In Andrew Sayer's clear formulation, the ideas described above mean that:

> The nature or constitution of an object and its causal powers are internally or necessarily related: a plane can fly by virtue of its aerodynamic form, engines, etc.; ... multinational firms can sell their products dear and buy their labour cheap by virtue of operating in several countries with different levels of development; people can change their behaviour by virtue of their ability to monitor their own monitorings; and so on. If the nature of an object changes then its causal powers will change too; engines lose their power as they wear out, a child's cognitive powers increase as it grows.
>
> (Sayer, 1992: 105)

One of the main consequences of the adoption of the conception of causal law above is that the explanation requires an explanatory model distinct from the deductive–nomological one described by Hempel (1965) and which is implicitly rejected by Boudon when he refuses to explain a particular educational structure purely on the basis of statistical relations which point to the constant conjunction between events. Contrary to the Hempelian model of explanation, Boudon recognises the need to identify certain mechanisms which generate the relations in question: the reasons of individuals. However, differently from the critical realists, Boudon does not consider the possibility of treating social structures as a type of agent, i.e. as an object which has the power to change something (including itself) (Bhaskar, 1997). For this reason, the causal powers of the social structure are not considered as such, but as mere methodological devices.

A realist interpretation of the model of education developed by Boudon would entail a conclusion not very different from his own, but it would take seriously the existence of the social structure and their causal powers: there is a (structural) tendency for low status individuals to be low achievers at school, but this tendency is not always actualised because the causal powers of certain individuals (high IQ, verbal achievement, etc.) may neutralise the causal powers of the social structure, thus leading to a transformation of that structure. This interpretation of the structure–agency relation in Boudon's model of education does not aim at showing any 'hidden meaning' which he did not perceive but, at the risk of sounding somewhat pretentious, at showing that the individualistic conclusions which he attributed to it and which were particularly emphasised in a later phase of his career do not strictly correspond to his actual analyses. What the model of education expounded here explicitly shows is that there is no deterministic relation between two structural variables and, in this sense, it emphasises the importance of human action in the explanation of social phenomena. The conclusion that structural variables are merely an aggregation of individual actions and the consequent individualistic conception of social structure is the result of an 'inflation' of the importance attributed to the notion of action given his refusal to consider seriously the existence of social structures based on their causal powers or on the effects they generate.

The paradox of this conclusion lies in the fact that certain causal powers are (heuristically) attributed to things whose existence is denied. In this sense, the consideration that social structures are merely descriptive propositions which have no explanatory power can only mean, according to Boudon's own definition of structure described in Chapter 1, that the theory which explained the emergence of a particular educational structure is either not 'strong enough' to ascertain its objective existence, or that social scientific activity is not a cumulative enterprise in the sense that its previous findings cannot be taken for granted in the explanation of new, unexplained phenomena.

The importance of Boudon's model of education for the subsequent development of his individualistic approach can be attributed to his conclusion that structural analysis has a heuristic character and that social phenomena have to be explained in terms of the actors' reasons for acting. As he recognised, 'it is particularly after *L'Inégalité des Chances* that I perceived the heuristic rather than explanatory role of causal analysis' (Boudon, 1986a: 314). Another important aspect of that book is that it poses problems of rationality and choice which later makes him shift the focus from the problem of the correspondence between two structural variables (and how they have to be mediated by the notion of action) to problems related to decisions taken at the individual or micro level and the structural outcome of their aggregation. This characterises what I have called the intermediate phase.[3]

The intermediate phase: perverse effects and social order

Perverse effects refer to what are commonly termed 'unintended consequences of social action' or, in Popper's terms (*apud* Boudon, 1982:1), 'non-intentional social repercussions of intentional human actions'. Although the term perverse effects is somewhat unfortunate, for it suggests undesirable effects, Boudon is very emphatic in stressing that it refers to both undesired desirable effects and undesired undesirable effects. For this reason, the term perverse effect is sometimes replaced by 'effect of composition' or 'aggregation effect', but each of them is taken by Boudon to have its own drawbacks: whereas the first is not particularly informative, the second suggests a concept from normative economics which is too strictly associated with the notion of *Homo economicus*. In later texts (see Boudon, 1981), the same idea is expressed in terms of emergent effects.[4] In spite of the terminological problems described above, all those terms deal with 'individual and collective effects that result from the juxtaposition of individual behaviours and yet were not included in the actor's explicit objectives' (Boudon, 1982:5).

Perverse effects are at the centre of the structure–agency problematic and, once again, it emphasises the non-deterministic aspects of social explanation:

> A perverse effect can only occur in an analytic framework in which the sociological subject, *Homo sociologicus*, is thought to be moved by the objectives he has in mind and the way he represents their eventual realisation to himself. ... There is ... a fundamental incompatibility between this paradigm and the contemporary paradigm of a *homo sociologicus* whose actions would have no more reality than that of responses determined by social 'structures'.
>
> (Boudon, 1982: 7)[5]

These effects are presented as an important form of social change, albeit not the only one, and its influence can be felt in everyday life situations, in the logic of collective action, in institutional change, etc. In order to illustrate this generality, Boudon works with three main types of examples: examples from everyday life, fictitious examples in the form of models and examples taken from empirical data, real facts, etc. Some authors have argued that this lack of homogeneity affects the demonstrative value of the examples to the extent that they are sometimes used to justify the centrality of perverse effects even when they are not fully justified (see Favre, 1980). Take, for instance, the example extracted from one of James Coleman's tables relating to an Index of Residential Segregation in Terms of Race. This table refers to the study of 109 North American towns between 1940 and 1960, and it shows that, during this period, there was an increase in the residential segregation and also an increase in the percentage of Whites who approved of residential integration. Boudon interprets such data in terms of a contradiction:

> [T]he existence of segregated housing does not represent what people in general feel, i.e. some fervent wish for life in a neighbourhood composed of people belonging to the same racial group. It represents, rather, an effect of composition. In choosing a home individuals consider first of all their means and their preferences as to kinds of housing. But suppose we push the argument further and posit that they attach *no* significance whatsoever to the ethnic composition of their environment. It is still a simple matter to show that effects of segregation may appear. These

would be the *undesired* result of the composition of choices made in a context in which availability of resources and ethnic affiliation are statistically linked.

(Boudon, 1982: 168–9)

According to Favre (1980), the interpretation of this table as a perverse effect results perhaps from Boudon's inability to identify a common phenomenon in social research, namely the divorce between the practices of individuals and the stereotyped answers collected in surveys. I believe, however, that this does not invalidate the importance of viewing certain types of structure as a result of perverse effects. This is particularly true if one considers that there is no reason why one should assume that most answers represent stereotyped answers, and not what people really believe. Moreover, given that Boudon does not take the subjects' accounts of reality to be necessarily true, this does not invalidate the fact that false accounts of reality may have a real effect on behaviour. In this sense, instead of adopting this line of argument, which seems to be based on the non-generality of perverse effects in social change, I shall concentrate on showing that there is a fundamental difference between perceiving structures as the result of the aggregation of action (which may bring about some emergent effect), and assuming that structures are always reducible to the aggregation of individual actions.

The Unintended Consequences of Social Action (1982) is a compilation of articles in which Boudon sketches the importance of perverse effects for sociological theory and, in my view, it does not pose any particular problems in terms of social theorising. It is in *La Logique du Social* (1979) and in other articles from the same period that he draws the full theoretical implications of this idea. In that book, he identifies two main elements involved in the generation of perverse effects (apart, of course, from action itself). The first is the type of structure or system which precedes action: functional systems and systems of interdependence. The second is the notion of situation.

Functional systems are defined as systems of interaction whose main category is roles. Systems of interdependence, on the other hand, are 'those systems of interaction where individual actions can be analysed without reference to the category of roles' (Boudon, 1981: 255). This distinction is actually another formulation for the distinction established earlier between *state of nature* and *context of contract*.

The notion of situation, in its turn, is the most vague, and yet, in my opinion, the most fertile of the concepts used by Boudon. He refers to 'the logic of the situation' in a number of books and articles (1979, 1981, 1982, 1984), but he never defines the term 'situation'. In the phrase in question, most of the time the concept is identical to the notion of structure or system of interaction, such as in his definition of open situation:

Let us imagine an interaction system of two people. They have repeatedly chosen between two options, A and B. Each can autonomously choose either A or B. According to their choices, they can contribute to the appearance of four situations: AA (the first has chosen A, the second has chosen A), AB (the first has chosen A, the second, B), BA (the first has chosen B, the second, A) and BB (the first has chosen B and the second has chosen B). ... [T]he situation ... is the result of the choice of two people who are autonomous in relation to each other.

(Boudon, 1984: 165–6)

According to this definition, the situation is considered as a set of interactions which can be analytically distinguished, that is, it is reducible to interactions or to reciprocal relations between actions. The same idea can be found in his definition of closed situations, and the differentiation between open/closed situations or systems of interdependence/functional systems is that the lower the margin of autonomy of the individual, the smaller the chances of perverse effects. This does not mean that perverse effects are restricted to systems of interdependence. In the first place, roles are always interpreted by the agents, which may give rise to unintended consequences. In the second place, 'the sociologist encounters what we have called systems of interdependence underlying all "organisations" or functional systems' (Boudon, 1984: 281). However, Boudon rightly stresses that systems of interdependence are richer in those effects:

[T]he transition from an unorganised system to an organised system is often due to the manifest will of social agents to eliminate undesirable emergent effects. On the other hand, it is clear that a process of organisation inevitably implies the introduction of norms and constraints which restrict the margin of individual autonomy and, therefore, include certain categories of actions in *roles*.

(Boudon, 1981: 257)

Apart from the identification of the notion of situation with social systems or social structures, this particular phase of Boudon's work is also characterised by the fact that social systems, particularly organised social systems, tend to be perceived as external constraints to action. It is, however, important to recognise that structures do not only constrain action, but also enable it. Therefore, norms cannot be viewed only in terms of external constraints, but also as belonging to 'the elements determining the choice within the area of freedom left open by the constraints' (Blegvad, 1979: 320). Although Boudon insists that action is always the result of choice, the differentiation between systems of interdependence and functional systems is made in a way which suggests a strict opposition between structure and freedom. This opposition, if taken strictly, leads either to a negation of the influence of structural factors on action (and thus action is always self-caused), or to the view that there is no place for action whenever there is an influence of structural factors. This is, however, clearly not the case in his analyses, and his attempt to develop what he calls a 'well-tempered determinism' leads to a particular attempt to reconcile individual freedom and the constraining aspects of social structures. Boudon tries to reconcile individual freedom and social 'determinism' by defining the role of structures in social explanation. In this attempt, he argues that it is through systems of interdependence that one can best understand the sense of Durkheim's intuitions, namely the *external* and *objective* character of the social structure and how it relates to individual agency:

> These systems [of interdependence] are exclusively subject to the will of the agents who constitute them. Nevertheless, everything occurs as if the consequences of their actions escaped their control: the division of labour, the nuclearization of the family, the oligarchic character of democratic parties, and anomie are not the consequence of anyone's will. These phenomena impose themselves on individuals in such a way that they appear to them as the product of anonymous forces. However, these immaterial forces are simply projections of structures of interdependence. *These structures cannot be reduced to the individuals who compose them.* This is the case, not only because generally the agents involved in a situation of interdependence have not directly chosen the institutions that define it, but also because *the collection of individuals constitutes a totality that is irreducible to the sum of its parts.* But, on the other hand, structures are nothing without individuals. [My emphasis]
>
> (Boudon, 1981: 281)

This definition shows one of the most fundamental paradoxes of Boudon's methodological individualism: if it is shown that perverse effects are the result of the aggregation of actions and that this result is irreducible to what was aggregated, in the sense that it presents some properties which cannot be found in any particular agent or, in Margaret Archer's words (1995), in any of the individuals present here and now, then social structures necessarily have an ontological status which guarantees a certain autonomy in relation to action. But if this autonomy is viewed exclusively in terms of an 'inhibiting environment' whose presence is felt 'through the pressurising effects which condition (actors') conduct' (Giddens, 1979: 51), then there is little place for action in social explanation. The problem is how Boudon can recognise the relative autonomy of the social structure and still account for what Giddens calls 'agent causality'. This is dealt with in the development of the notion of situation.

The integration of structure and action calls for an account of norms and rules in terms of a theory of motivation, and this theory has to provide a link between objective and subjective elements. This is where the notion of situation, as something which may be distinct from the social structure, comes into play. In the most recent phase of his work, the notion of situation can be used not only as the equivalent of social and cultural systems, but also of certain properties of individuals which arise out of the relations between structure and agency.

The most recent phase: the study of ideas

The most recent phase of Boudon's work can roughly be characterised by the development of a theory of rationality in which the explanation of beliefs assumes a central role. In terms of the agency–structure problem, this can be generally translated into the question of how the social structure and the social situation affect beliefs, knowledge and, in a more indirect way, action. This does not mean that there was a change of focus to action as the effect, rather than the cause of social structures, but simply that a certain account of the social structure, social situation, etc., is required for the understanding and explanation of those collective beliefs which ground social action. The theory of rationality which he developed with this aim particularly emphasises those cases in which beliefs cannot be taken for granted in the explanation of social phenomena, but have to be taken as dependent variables if any sense is to be made of the actions involved. The study of the origin of ideas includes both false or fragile, and true or solid beliefs. In addition, this phase of his work deals with the explanation of beliefs relating to both a positive or descriptive domain, and to a normative or prescriptive one. The former are dealt with mainly in *L'Idéologie* (1986a) and in *L'Art de se Persuader* (1990a), and the latter in *Le Juste et le Vrai* (1995a) and *Le Sens de Valeurs* (1999a).

A word of warning needs to be given here. The central axis of Boudon's explanation of beliefs rests on a theory of rationality which will be discussed in detail in Chapter 3. This means that the relations between structure and agency which are being investigated now have to be regarded as a rough sketch. I believe, however, that this sketch may represent a useful tool in the analysis of his theory of cognitive rationality. Given this, I will try to limit myself here to the structure–agency problematic, leaving, whenever possible, problems related to rationality to be analysed in Chapter 3.

According to Boudon (1986a), the purpose of *L'Idéologie* is to show that individualistic methods can be adopted in the explanation of collective beliefs. As usual, the meaning of action is of fundamental importance: 'to analyse a subject's adherence to an ill founded idea, is to understand the meaning this idea presents to him. In other words, it is to make it evident the reasons he has for adopting it' (ibid.: I).[6]

Ideology is defined by Boudon in terms of false knowledge, which does not mean that the concept is reducible to illegitimate arguments in scientific terms, although this can also be the case. Ideologies are viewed instead as a normal product of scientific knowledge, because the models developed to explain reality are always imperfect. In this sense, they are often the result of a realist (essentialist) interpretation of models which are themselves more or less remote from reality.

Apart from trying to show that ideologies are a normal ingredient of social life, Boudon also tries to show that they are produced not despite social actors being rational, but *because* they are rational. Ideologies are considered as 'understandable' ideas in the Weberian sense of understanding, i.e. as more or less rational phenomena in which irrationality assumes a residual role in their explanation insofar as ideologies do not merely have the function of covering and dissimulating passions and feelings. Although Boudon does not deny the existence of collective passions and feelings, or that ideologies may present a covering up function, he argues that, when it comes to believing in certain false ideas, cognitive aspects assume an essential role: agents can like or dislike others, like or dislike a flag, etc., but they do not believe in a theory because they like it. In this sense, instead of treating cognitive error as a direct consequence of passions and feelings, the relations between these things are mediated by genuinely cognitive processes. It is in this sense that, in a later work, he approvingly quotes J.S. Mill's idea that 'every erroneous inference, though originating in moral causes, involves the intellectual operation of admitting insufficient evidence as sufficient' (Mill *apud* Boudon, 1990a: 53).

In order to grasp the meaning of ideologies, Boudon considers it necessary to take actors as situated, which means that they do not see the world in the same way from all view points. In addition to that, it is necessary to consider that whether actors perceive the world from a particular view point depends on what they know and also on what they do not know. This is summarised in a category which Boudon calls situation effects. Here it is possible to perceive that the notion of situation refers not only to external phenomena, but also to subjective or cognitive elements. Situation effects comprise both position (objective) and disposition (subjective) effects and, through their influence, the social actor tends to perceive reality not as it is or in the same way that others perceive it, but in a partial or deformed way:

> It is evident that what I see here and now depends on my location in space. We do not see the same thing from the front yard as we see from the garden, and what I see from the front yard particularly depends on what I already know, such as the fact that a beautiful neighbour or a cantankerous couple inhabits the flat across the street.
>
> (Boudon, 1986a: 106)[7]

Naturally, the notion of position refers to the social position of the actor and it may engender other kinds of effects, like perspective effects, and role effects. The notion of disposition, in its turn, refers to the intentionalities of the actors in a broad Husserlian sense, i.e. the way towards which attention is directed: 'dispositions are the cognitive resources, the knowledge which we have acquired and can make use of' (Boudon, 1986a: 301).[8] He also admits that the word disposition may have a non-cognitive sense, and when he refers to affective or traditional aspects of dispositions, he sometimes uses the notion of *habitus*, taking great care to differentiate the sense that this notion assumes for him and for Pierre Bourdieu. According to him, the 'good definitions' of *habitus* are those of Aristotle, Thomas Aquinas, Wittgenstein and Ryle. Contrary to Bourdieu's notion, Boudon argues, these definitions do not exclude a certain degree of voluntarism in action, do not assume it to be unconscious, do not have a fixed content, do not assume dispositions to be mechanical, do not take them to be determined in an exclusively social manner and do not consider them as fully determined by the position of the actors in the stratification system.

Another category of effects developed by Boudon for the analysis of ideology is that of communication effects. This category is closely related to the concept of authority, in the sense that certain ideas are taken to be true because people who are considered to be experts on that particular subject take them to be true. In order to illustrate this process, Boudon makes use of the cybernetic notions of white and black boxes. Since certain dispositions (or cognitive resources) are associated with a particular social position, certain ideas are often treated as black, rather than white boxes. This is because instead of taking up the costs involved in specialised knowledge, it can be more 'rational' from an individual point of view not to look for what is behind that knowledge, but rather to take an idea to be true because those who are taken to be competent in that domain take it to be true. In this sense, an authority effect is developed whenever the public involved in a communication relation does not dispose of the resources and necessary competence to treat the theory or idea in question as a white box.

Finally, there is a third category of effects to which those who produce ideologies are subject: epistemological effects. These effects are derived from the a priori notions, frames of reference or paradigms which the knowing subject uses when apprehending reality. Boudon's main argument in the characterisation of epistemological effects is that both the lexicon and the paradigms of science are full of 'a priori forms', i.e. of notions which are considered self-evident or well enough accepted to be taken for granted, even when they are mistaken. Although concepts, paradigms, theories, etc., are what guide scientific activity, sometimes their epistemological status as a priori forms is mistaken for a realist description of reality, and their applicability is not questioned enough or tends to be extended outside their scope.

In order to illustrate how Boudon analyses ideology according to the three types of effects just described, I will summarise one of his case studies. This case study focuses on developmentalism, for Boudon, an ideology according to which Western countries have the capacity and the responsibility to develop underdeveloped countries.

With the aim of answering the question of how developmentalism established itself and became such a widely accepted theory, he starts by noting that from the 1950s to the 1970s a number of specialists on socio-economic development proposed converging theories which concluded that development depended on external aid. The most influential of these theories was Nurkse's theory of the vicious circle, which is summarised by Boudon (1986a: 248) in the following statements:

1   In poor countries, the possibilities of saving are weak.
2   Consequently, the possibilities of investing are weak.
3   Increased productivity normally results from capital investments.
4   Because investments are low, it is difficult to achieve gains in productivity.
5   The increase in the quality of life depends on increasing productivity.
6   Because gains in productivity are unlikely to happen in poor countries, quality of life and savings stagnate.
7   Because development cannot happen in an endogenous way, it has to be induced by external aid and by the injection of foreign capital.

According to Boudon's theoretical scheme, the main reason for the appeal of this theory lies in epistemological effects. First, it accords with the traditional canons of scientificity: not only has it a general explanatory power, but it is made up of a set of propositions which can be taken as true either because they represent analytical propositions in the Kantian sense, or because they represent some sort of empirical commonplace. Second, because so many theories which led to more or less the same conclusions were being produced at the time, they were subject to a convergence effect according to which each of these theories added credibility to the others.

In addition to epistemological effects, the credibility of development theories can be attributed to sociological reasons which give rise to 'powerful communication effects'. During the period in which these theories were conceived, the world was dominated by Western countries, mainly the United States. The 'Third World' was not conceived as a political actor on the international scene, and the idea that development could only happen through external aid was in accordance with this world view. Moreover, the theories produced by 'underdeveloped' countries were either dependent on the theories produced in developed countries or, when they were in fact original, they had a restricted influence.

A close analysis of the propositions of this vicious circle theory show, nonetheless, that the credibility that it received was ill founded. Boudon tries to show that a number of invisible parameters and hypotheses lay under its propositions. Its main proposition, which states that, in poor countries, the possibilities of saving are weak, does not take into account that these countries are normally characterised by great inequality. They therefore have, by definition, a minority which has the possibility of saving. In this sense, a proposition which has the appearance of an analytical statement is in fact a proposition which has to be empirically grounded.

Another proposition advanced by the vicious circle theory states that an increase in productivity is normally achieved through the substitution of labour by fixed capital. According to Boudon, this is an empirical generalisation of a phenomenon which is characteristic of developed societies only. In developing societies, where the primary sector is preponderant, increased productivity is generated by other means, such as the modification of agricultural methods, or a redistribution of tasks within the production system. The generalisation and acceptance of a proposition which is true for industrialised countries only results from a sociocentric reference which is translated by him in terms of a perspective effect, a sub-category of position effects.

There are a number of other implicit hypotheses upon which the validity of the theory of the vicious circle rests and which are not justified. For example, there is a tacit assumption that the societies which it describes do not have significant external exchanges. If such an assumption was not made, one would have to consider that the societies in question could, for instance, benefit from an increase in productivity from abroad.

Despite the generality of this description, it is clear that the main element in Boudon's theory of ideology is the 'situatedness' of the social actor, which he summarises in the following passage:

> The sociologist may consider the social actors as rational. And he has indeed an advantage in doing so, if we agree with Max Weber. But, at the same time, he should draw all the consequences from the fact that the social actors are socially situated, that is to say, that they have social roles, that they belong to certain social environments and societies, that they dispose of certain resources (especially cognitive ones), and that, due to the socialisation processes they were subject to, they have *interiorised* a certain amount of knowledge and representations. For these reasons, they are subject to what I have called situation (position and disposition) effects.
>
> (Boudon, 1986a: 137)[9]

The way in which a situation is dealt with in the analysis of ideology seems, however, to overlook some problems in the relation between the position and dispositions of actors. Possibly in order to deny that there is a necessary and sufficient relation between positions and dispositions, Boudon eliminates an important category from the study of ideology: power. Take, for instance, the perspective effect described in his case study (increase in productivity is achieved through the substitution of labour by fixed capital). This perspective effect is then taken to be generalised through sociocentrism. But how does a sociocentric perspective from developed countries affect the self-perception of 'underdeveloped' countries, thus making it possible for their adoption of false ideas from abroad? Perception is not a direct, unmediated phenomenon, and the very idea of (social) perspective includes a number of elements other than individual cognitive abilities. Perception is a function of intentionality (in the sense defined above, i.e. in the sense of cognitive resources), but it is also a function of the actors' abilities to manipulate and deceive others, a function which is not completely accounted for in the category of authority. This points to an important limit to the explanatory power of his theory of ideology to the extent that his emphasis on the cognitive dimension of dispositions affects the account of communication effects. For instance, if the idea that theories produced in 'underdeveloped' countries have a restricted influence is not attributed to a direct link between underdevelopment and lack of scientific competence, then it has to be considered that scientific authority does not rest on cognitive resources only. Any account of communication effects has to take into account power relations which do not necessarily rest on conscious psychological processes (which is implied in his definition of authority). This is particularly true if one takes into account that power relations are based not only in establishing what is true, but also what is considered to be important and 'marketable'. Of course, if one of the actors is not recognised as such, as Boudon suggests about the Third World, then the aforementioned process is implicitly accounted for. I believe, however, that the model could benefit from an explicit consideration of such processes which can be described under the category of power.

L'Art de se Persuader (Boudon, 1990a) can be considered as the development of one of the effects described in *L'Ideologie*: epistemological effects. Differently from what happens in *L'Idéologie*, the notion is now used to account for cognitive processes that happen both within and outside scientific activity. Epistemological effects can be generally described as the process through which unacceptable conclusions are drawn from solid premises, thus characterising it as a process which happens in everyday life as much as in science. This leads to a theory of rationality which accounts for beliefs by considering them as the result of the (non-objectively) good reasons which actors have for believing in them. The notion of good reasons as an explanatory element rules out the idea that social actors are always driven by forces which escape their own subjective evaluation of their situation, although Boudon does not deny that some affective causes may enter the explanation of beliefs: 'I by no means consider that all beliefs should be explained by reasons. ... it is also true that many beliefs have affective causes, whether they are observable or not.' (Boudon, 1990a: 46).[10] However, this concession to affective causes of behaviour does not imply any concession to determinism, for, even here, there is an element of subjectivity and rationality which accords centrality to action. In other words, Boudon insists on the superiority of an explanation of human behaviour in which reasons represent an important type of cause.

The central idea developed here is that the reasons an actor has to adopt a certain belief may be either objectively or merely 'subjectively' good, and it is in the work of G. Simmel that Boudon finds an important source of 'good reasons' for believing in fragile or false ideas. This is developed into a model, the 'Simmelian model', which rests on Simmel's main epistemological positions and which is described as follows.[11]

According to Boudon (1990a), Simmel accepts the Kantian principle that knowledge is not a copy of reality, but that it presupposes an active intervention of the subject in the production of knowledge through the mediation of a priori notions. On the other hand, Simmel does not agree with the inflexible character of the Kantian a priori notions, and suggests that they are more numerous and more variable, both in time and space, than Kant believed. These a priori notions represent a kind of framework for thought, and are perceived by the subject only in a 'metaconscious' way. Moreover, they are considered as self-evident enough not to be questioned in every situation. Neo-Kantian a priori notions thus play a fundamental role in the production of knowledge, rendering it possible, on the one hand, but also generating false notions about reality. The main idea developed in the Simmelian model is that:

> A perfectly valid argumentation may lead to false conclusions to the extent that we do not perceive the implicit propositions involved, and that we are not conscious of the fact that our conclusions *also* derive from these implicit propositions which we tacitly adopt because we have good reasons to adopt them.
>
> (Boudon, 1990a: 60–1)[12]

Good reasons are defined by Boudon very much in accord with the commonsense definition of the term, and the philosophical definition of good reasons as objectively good does not apply here. Good reasons can be objectively 'bad', but subjectively good. Nonetheless, subjectively good reasons are neither arbitrary nor dependent on the subject's idiosyncrasies, but tend to be general, in the sense that all individuals who are placed in the same situation will perceive the same reasons as good. This is strictly linked to the idea that, whenever social actors are confronted with a problem, they mobilise some a priori notions or conjectures which are taken for granted in everyday life.

This distinction calls for a model of rationality conceived in terms of the actors' situation. Situated or contextual rationality is thus the category which accounts for the link between situation (position and disposition) and belief (or action). Any proper analysis of this link has to consider in detail the rationality model involved and, even though this will be left for Chapter 3, it is already possible to observe the establishment of a much more complex link between the objective and subjective aspects of social phenomena than in some of his previous analyses.

Whereas *L' Art de se Persuader* deals with the explanation of positive beliefs, that is, beliefs about the world as it is, *Le Juste et le Vrai* also deals with normative beliefs, or beliefs relative to what ought to be. The concern with normative beliefs leads Boudon to develop Max Weber's notion of axiological rationality, which is interpreted as a consequence of Weber's methodological rule of explaining social phenomena through reasons. This type of explanation involves, as we have already seen, a reconstruction of the actors' reasons, and this reconstruction is what guarantees, in his paradigm of action, the movement between action (or beliefs) and structure (or social position). Contrary to what was implied in the intermediate phase of his work, an explanation of the actors' reasons is neither conceived in voluntaristic terms, nor, when it takes the social structure into account, merely in terms of constraint.

Despite his continuing adherence to methodological individualism, it should be noted that Boudon focuses especially on collective beliefs, and the collective character of both positive and normative beliefs is viewed as a consequence of the objectivity of the reasons which lie at their foundation. Whereas individual beliefs have to be interpreted in terms of the meaning that they have for a certain individual, collective beliefs are the result of the reasons that any individual placed in a given place in the social structure has for adopting them. In addition to dealing with collective beliefs, Boudon considers that certainty about a belief is stronger, the stronger is the system of reasons at its root; and cognitive mechanisms are viewed as an important source of certainty. Characteristically enough, these ideas are interpreted in terms of the aggregation of individual beliefs, in the sense that they constitute reasons that all perceive as strong enough: 'insofar as the sociologist is interested in collective beliefs, we should stipulate that this subjective meaning tends to be shared by those who find themselves in the same situation' (Boudon, 1995a: 94).[13] Certainly, this definition of individual is most suspect to the extent that what is at stake here is not really an individual person, but the more general concept of social agent.

Apart from maintaining the 'individualistic' characterisation of social explanation, the model of rationality developed here is no different from that of *L'Art de se Persuader*: 'False beliefs are the product of "cognitive rationality", that is, of the subject's adoption of certain strategies, which are normally used in order to obtain a cognitive matrix of the environment because they normally lead to satisfactory results.' (ibid.: 107).[14] This cognitivist approach is opposed to what Boudon refers to as 'causalism'. According to him, there are two main categories of causes which are preferred by 'causalists': affective causes and social causes. Without denying the importance and validity of explanations based on affective causes, Boudon believes that this type of explanation tends to be overrated and extended to domains where an explanation by reasons would be more appropriate. In any case, the opposition he establishes is against 'emotionalism', in the sense of a causal relation which goes from effect to reasons. For him, in moral feelings, causality usually runs from reasons to feelings, and:

> It is no longer a matter of denying that, in the majority of cases, affective and rational elements are inseparably associated. The feeling of indignation which we experience when an elderly person is deprived of her resources by a dishonest relative is based on universal reasons. It is because that feeling rests on reasons that are immediately understood by anyone that it is experienced in a particularly strong way on the affective level. Even though those reasons are presented to the subjects' consciousness in a rather imperfect way, they are in fact the cause of the subjects' reactions and of the feeling they generate.
>
> (Boudon, 1995a: 169)[15]

Social causalism or determinism would be another adversary of explanation through reasons. This approach takes socialisation as the main, if not the sole, cause of beliefs and actions. Boudon's contention with this sort of explanation is that, although he emphasises that both beliefs and actions tend to vary in time, space, circumstances and the social context in general, this dependence on the social situation is not valid in itself: the force of conviction comes not from socialisation, but from the actors' faith that the beliefs and actions are founded on reasons which can be argued for.

How does Boudon account for the reasons on which actions and beliefs are based? One possible way would be to characterise social actors as rational, in the sense that they always try to maximise their interests or their preferences. But Boudon basically disagrees with this solution, for he recognises the fact that this approach presupposes a conscious relation between means and ends, and that there are a number of actions which are inspired by metaconscious reasons and which do not have any particular (instrumental) end. The reduction of all types of action to a very particular one (instrumental rationality), leads to a theory of human action which is not just abstract, but unrealistic. A more realistic theory has to take into account that reasons derive more or less directly from a conjunction of empirical, logical and moral principles and facts, some of which are universal, others which are contextually indexed. In summary, it has to take into account all the elements which are considered to be relevant to explanation, and which Boudon summarises by the abstract notion of situation. Because these elements vary according to the kind of phenomenon to be explained and the questions to be answered, a concrete definition of the situation cannot be given in advance but has to be constructed in each case. And the link between these elements of the situation (including the social structure) and action or belief, is established through a notion of rationality which is context related (cognitive rationality).

The thesis according to which normative judgements rest on the same cognitive processes as positive ones is developed further in his *Le Sens de Valeurs* (Boudon, 1999a), a collection of essays dealing with the contemporary responses to the question of why we believe in certain ideas and whether they belong in the realm of science, morality or aesthetics. Most of these responses share a common trait, though in varying degrees: relativism. Some of these relativistic responses rest on a radical split between the positive and the normative dimensions, leading to the idea that feelings of justice escape any attempt to theorisation; others rest on a more general mistrust of notions such as truth and objectivity. This last idea is explained through the influence of a mechanism which Boudon identifies with the help of Tocqueville's works and which constitutes a particularly interesting case of perverse effect. This mechanism is called the Tocqueville effect.

Among the many factors responsible for the transformation of relativism into an essential cultural trait of contemporary society, Boudon identifies a long-term and irreversible one: a general and dominant passion, present in democratic societies, known as the principle of equality. According to this value, all groups and cultures must be treated as equal. However, given that individuals are placed in cultural settings which subscribe to different values, the only way of remaining faithful to that principle is by admitting that there is neither truth nor objectivity when it comes to values other than equality. Accordingly, they must be regarded as mere view points.

The generality of such a value accounts for the fact that, even if particular individuals are not convinced of its truth, people tend to adhere to it, particularly when the alternative values at stake do not directly concern them. This happens as an effect of the tyranny of opinion which, for Boudon, does not necessarily mean that individuals do not preserve their freedom of judgement rather it is taken to mean that, even though the dominant character which an opinion assumes may not be enough to ground its truth, it may be enough to confer it a high degree of influence. In other words, for Tocqueville, in contrast to philosophers such as Nietzsche, relativism is considered not as an indisputable truth, but as a point of view which tends to impose itself on individuals under certain social and historical conditions (Boudon, 1999a: 304). Under these conditions, Boudon identifies a number of convergent effects, such as the de-colonisation process which took place in modern societies and which helped to discredit evolutionism; the development of minorities' rights; the crisis of Marxism and its end as an important ideology; the crisis of the universities and the orientation of knowledge towards the media (which tends to value aesthetic and economic, rather than cognitive aspects), etc.

Nonetheless, the force of the Tocqueville effect is limited and sometimes neutralised by other effects, with the result that it sometimes does not manifest itself. In an important sense, there is a limit to both relativism and scepticism, for they cannot assume an absolute dimension without posing serious threats to social life. A certain degree of consensus in relation to a minimal set of values is a basic condition of social life. In addition to that, Boudon argues that it is possible that certain societies are viewed as both grounded on a large degree of consensus and strongly attached to equalitarian values, which would refute Tocqueville's opposition between equalitarianism and consensus about the truth or righteousness of particular values. Such seems to be the case of the United States during the post-war period: '[T]he horrors of the Second World War engendered a consensus about democratic values, whereas the tensions of the cold war stimulated a congregation effect around the fundamental values of the American nation.' (Boudon, 1999a: 306).[16] Rather than refuting Tocqueville's theory, Boudon sees this example as imposing limits and establishing possibilities of its manifestation: such consensus may be fragile, circumstantial and, sometimes, more apparent than real (and the strong explosion of the 'free speech movement' confirms this impression). In this sense, the lack of manifestation of Tocqueville's effect is not enough to deny its existence in terms of a fundamental mechanism for the dissemination of relativism, but, in a typically realist argument, such lack of manifestation must be seen as a particular instance where a relation does not obtain 'because it is counteracted by the presence of particular factors' (ibid.: 307).[17]

In terms of the structure–agency problem, the Tocquevillian effect illustrates a fundamental aspect of social explanation which is either denied or, at best, minimised by Boudon's methodological individualism: the fact that, despite the social structure's intrinsic dependence on human agency, there are emergent phenomena in social life which cannot be seen as a mere synopsis of actions and/or beliefs. Rather, they refer to causal powers which cannot be reduced to those powers belonging to the individuals who compose a given social system at a given time and which, even when they are not actualised through human agency, remain potentially operative.

Concluding remarks

I argued in Chapter 1 that, although the structure–agency relation is not taken by Boudon to be a central issue in his methodology, it is in fact fundamental both for differentiating individualism from atomism and for emphasising the former's alleged epistemological status. While Boudon's methodological individualism is strictly opposed to sociologism (in the sense of those approaches which explain social phenomena solely by reference to structural elements), it does not deny the importance of structures for the understanding of action. Nevertheless, the emphasis on a purely explanatory individualism (if that is at all possible) does not do away with the old debate about the status of collective concepts.

This was shown in this chapter through an analysis of how the notion of structure was dealt with in different phases of his work. In the first phase, represented here by his analysis of education, the explanation rested mainly on the effects a given social structure had on individual preferences and some general dispositions, and how the individual actions which followed from those preferences affected that very social structure (in the sense of transforming and/or maintaining certain structural traits). The idea that the effects of a certain structure can only be determined through the effects it has on the actions of individual agents makes Boudon consider that relations between two structural elements are not really causal, but merely an explanatory device which summarises the effects actions taken at a time t_1 have on actions at t_2.

This idea is extended and developed in his account of social change as the effect of unintended consequences of intentional actions (perverse effects). The importance the notion of perverse effects assumes in the development of his individualism can probably be attributed to the idea that, even when the result of the aggregation of action is not in accordance with what was intended by individual agents, it is still the result of individual actions.

When dealing with the generative elements of perverse effects, Boudon reintroduces the concept of structure and concludes that there is one particular type of structure which has the property of inducing agents to act in a certain way:

> Certain systems of interdependence induce social agents to undertake actions leading to what are, from their point of view, undesirable effects. It also indicates – this point is of particular importance – that, in certain situations, social agents can be aware of the undesirable effects that they incur, while at the same time being incapable of avoiding them.
>
> (Boudon, 1981: 260)

The external and objective character of social structures is then minimised though an explanatory approach which concentrates on the rational (*sensu lato*) character of action and the subsumption of that notion into the individual's situation. The notion of situation is accounted for in terms of a *description* of the individual's environment and inner states and, given that the dispositional aspects of the situation refer only to the level of agency, the explanation can only be granted if causality lies in the rational development of action.

This makes it evident that Boudon's main contention in relation to the use of collective concepts refers to his critique of the methodological rule of holistic explanations which 'try to locate macroscopic tendencies or relations and then treat them as sufficient causal explanations' (Boudon, 1995a: 180). Collective concepts have, for him, a descriptive, not an explanatory role, and their use as explanatory elements leads to an arbitrary interpretation of other people's behaviour to the extent that they ignore an important element of social life: human consciousness. It is the notion of action which accounts for that element, mainly the category of cognitive rationality. The reduction of collective concepts to actions thus refers to the need to consider human action as the only causal mechanism in social phenomena, and not to the nominalist rule of reduction of collective concepts to individual ones on the basis of empirical criteria. Nonetheless, as realists have extensively argued, one important criterion for the attribution of an entity's existence lies in causal criteria, and once both empirical and causal criteria are excluded, concepts assume a purely nominal or rhetorical character.

In fact, Boudon tries not to make any ontological statements about sociological concepts. Not even the concept of the individual escapes this rule. An individual is defined in terms of his/her situation and this definition represents a very abstract notion which only has relations with reality at the moment when it has been defined. This lack of ontological commitment raises a serious problem which was formulated by Giovanni Busino (1994: 48) in the following terms: Boudon's conception of sociology seems to rest on 'virtual facts', i.e. on objects which are adequately determined from the perspective of description, but undetermined from the perspective of empirical conditions. Contrary to Busino's view, the problem lies not so much with empirical criteria of existence, but with causal ones. In this sense, it is not difficult to see that concepts at the level of agency, because they relate to causal criteria of concept formation, do indeed present an ontological status that finds no equivalent in the realm of collective concepts. This is particularly true of Boudon's notion of (individuals') dispositions, which accounts for particular tendencies or powers which are intrinsic to particular objects.

But this denial of the causal powers of social structures is easier said than done. Although Boudon's methodological prescriptions rest on that kind of assumption, most of his substantive analyses constitute proof of the intrinsic weakness of such an approach to the extent that collective concepts are often 'smuggled' into his explanatory models in a real causal manner.

It is important to consider, however, that the action frame of reference developed by Boudon does indeed represent an important element in sociological theory. As William Outhwaite has pointed out, that frame of reference allows for the penetration, in a deep and precise way, into the way in which society exists only in individuals in definite social relations. But 'this is not because structures are unreal and only action theory has a legitimate foundation in a basic Strawsonian ontology of persons, but because, for certain purposes, this is the appropriate level of abstraction at which to operate.' (Outhwaite, 1987: 114). In this sense, it is worthwhile to notice that, despite the intrinsic relations between ontology and methodology, these two dimensions can, at least to a certain extent, be held apart. The problem arises when methodological aspects are extended to the ontological domain through considerations such as the merely descriptive, nominal or rhetorical character of all collective elements of analysis, or the idea of individualism as some sort of 'rock bottom explanation'.

Any attempt to rescue the epistemological value of the non-truistic aspects of individualism has to be made in terms of the maintenance of the notion of individual freedom, that is, on the assumption that individuals are not passive entities upon which social forces are necessarily imposed, and that the reasons of individuals do indeed represent an important causal mechanism in social phenomena, albeit not the only one. This constitutes the core of Boudon's theory of cognitive rationality, and the problem to which this leads me now refers to the understanding of how his definition and explanation of individual behaviour incorporates social predicates in his category of cognitive rationality and whether this incorporation solves the problem of an individualistic approach, i.e. the problem of how to account for belief, value and preference formation in general in terms of a non-realist account of social structures.

3 Beyond *Homo sociologicus* and *Homo economicus*

A complex theory of rationality

The model of rationality developed by Boudon represents the hard core of his methodology, since it aims at providing the basis for social explanation according to the principles of methodological individualism. This model attempts to integrate and go beyond two distinct approaches: one represented by a model of an actor conceived as *Homo sociologicus* and according to which social action is explained through the internalisation of norms and values; the other by *Homo economicus*, which emphasises the utilitarian aspects of action. This combination aims at social explanation through an action paradigm according to which action is neither 'a mechanical response to a given situation' nor defined by 'some external source of meaning such as a theory of history' (Outhwaite, 1996: 03).

The development of a rationality model is regarded by Boudon as a fundamental step towards a sociological theory which incorporates two basic epistemological issues for sociological analysis and which are closely related to the structure–agency problem. The first of these issues is what he calls 'Pareto's problem', the second, 'Durkheim's problem'. The former is defined by Boudon (1979) in terms of Pareto's most fundamental intuition: the notion of non-logical actions as a means of indicating the insufficiency of economic theories of action (utilitarian theories) for the explanation of a great number of social actions which, despite not fitting into the utilitarian model, are not irrational. Durkheim's intuition, on the other hand, refers to the role of sociology as the determination of how social structures 'orient' the behaviour of individuals.

The need to merge and relativise these two intuitions became particularly important for Boudon when he accounted for the difficulties and limitations presented by each of them. Pareto's notion of non-logical actions is particularly unclear because it rests on the boundaries of logical or rational actions and illogical or irrational ones. For Boudon, its lack of clarity comes from the very impossibility of giving a general definition of rationality, a notion which can only acquire a precise meaning when defined in terms of a particular context of interaction (or in terms of a particular situation). The Paretian social actor, *Homo economicus*, which is fundamentally active, thus becomes a problematic one, and this is where one feels the need to incorporate some of Durkheim's intuitions into the Paretian model. But insofar as Durkheim's methodology does not always allow for the consideration of the intentional aspects of actions, it may lead to a conception of *Homo sociologicus* as a passive subject, a sort of *automaton* whose behaviour is taken solely as the effect of social causes (Boudon, 1979: 37). The solution to this problem appears in the form of an attempt to define *Homo sociologicus* as both active and socially situated. Such a conception develops into a model of rationality which extends towards non-utilitarian aspects of behaviour, but which uses utilitarianism as a starting point.

Utilitarianism and the social sciences

Beyond its particular doctrines and theories, utilitarianism can be broadly defined as a cluster of theories which rests on the assumption that individuals are driven by individual pleasure. Although it is possible to distinguish utilitarianism as a theory of motivation, on the one hand, and as moral theory, on the other, I believe that these two aspects are intrinsically related, especially in its classical form, given that the former provides a model of the actor according to which morality is developed.

For Sen and Williams (1994), for instance, utilitarianism as a moral theory is the combination of two kinds of theory: welfarism and consequentialism. Welfarism is defined by them as 'a theory of the correct way to assess or assign value to states of affairs, and it claims that the correct basis of assessment is welfare, satisfaction, or people getting what they prefer'. Consequentialism, in its turn, is 'a theory of correct action, which claims that actions are to be chosen on the basis of the states of affairs which are their consequences.' (ibid.: 3). From this combination, utilitarianism in its basic form recommends a choice of action based on its consequences, which are then assessed in terms of welfare.

Without going into details of the history of utilitarian thought, it is important to bear in mind its influence when accounting for the development of modern academic disciplines such as economics and, to a lesser extent, sociology. According to Allan Caillé (1988), one of the main representatives of the Anti-Utilitarian Movement in the Social Sciences (MAUSS), utilitarianism is normally considered, in the history of thought, to be the philosophy of Jeremy Bentham, a philosophy which was later developed by his disciple James Mill and a number of other less well-known Anglo-Saxon philosophers.[1]

This rather restrictive view is contested by Caillé, for whom the philosophy developed by Bentham was merely a particular formulation of the utilitarian problematic implicit in all European thought after the Middle Ages. According to him, the origin of utilitarianism is related to the increasingly secular definition of justice as opposed to a definition in terms of authority and tradition. It probably starts with Thomas Aquinas' opposition between two distinct domains: that of supernatural theological nature, inaccessible to human reason; and the sphere of both the sacred Catholic Church and profane society. In this opposition, society is conceived as an association of people, bound together by their needs, and whose only aim is human welfare. This view, shared and developed by a number of other European thinkers, reaches its climax with theories of social contract.

Social contract theories represent a more or less strict utilitarian view, depending on the degree of identification between human practice, in general, and interests. In transferring the monopoly of legitimacy from God to the Prince or to the State, both Machiavelli and Hobbes, for instance, justified violence and ruse for the formation of the national state and viewed the social contract as the only means of assuring the attainment of human needs and desires. The Hobbesian view of the state, in particular, was already entirely utilitarian, and so was his idea of natural right, which was, according to Baker (1960: XIX), more properly a 'natural power or potentia' for the actor to do as he/she likes, irrespective of others. In fact, egoistic hedonism can be taken as a natural development of Hobbes's natural rights: 'we do not ... by nature seek society for its own sake, but that we may receive some honour or profit from it' (Hobbes, 1972: 33).

A counter movement was developed, following an attempt to distribute the monopoly of legitimacy from the Prince to other men. In this attempt, morality starts to be separated from the social sciences, but the true development from natural law into the social sciences took place in Scotland, with the political economy of Adam Smith. Developing the ideas of Hume and Hutcheson, he replaced interest by sympathy in his theory of morality. Sympathy, for Adam Smith, meant sharing the feeling produced in another person. Morality depends, thus, on these shared feelings and not on (shared) interests. This position goes against two main tenets of other forms of utilitarianism: egoism and rationalism. Although sympathy produces pleasure, the 'pleasure of mutual sympathy' (Smith, 1976: 13), the feeling of approval (or disapproval) of an action is the second, not the first, feeling produced. The first feeling in moral judgement can also be pain, since sympathy can be related either to pleasure or grief. This means that only secondarily is there utility in sympathy. For this reason, Caillé (1988) characterises utilitarianism in political economy as both 'dominant and balanced'.

The emergence of the social sciences is related to many of the findings of political economy. Through the work of Adam Smith, authors such as Malthus, Ricardo, J.S. Mill and Marx came to conclusions which questioned the rules that defined property rights, the distribution of income among different social classes and the division of labour (Hollis, 1976). For them, there could be no moral justification for these rules, and the emergence of the social sciences came with the recognition that individuals and the social relations that unite them constitute a separate domain from morality. This recognition led to the questioning of the nature of this domain, and the consequent emergence of both economics and sociology. Nonetheless, utilitarianism can still be seen as a dominant paradigm in the development of these sciences. Positive economics in particular, in breaking with the moral questioning of political economy, brought back the calculating actor of utilitarianism, only, this time, an amoral one. As Martin Hollis (1976: 48–9) has argued:

> In economics, the triumph of Positivism was the triumph of Utility. Man, illumined by the Enlightenment and anatomised by the utilitarians, was an individual bundle of desires. He was simply a complex animal, no less part of Nature than anything else and no less subject to discoverable empirical laws. His behaviour was to be explained as a series of attempts to get what he wanted. Whether his wants were metaphysical, religious, ethical or merely selfish was not to the point. For, scientifically speaking, it could simply be said that he was seeking the satisfaction of his desires. Judgements of value were irrelevant, except insofar as it could be asked scientifically whether the means chosen would secure the end, given the impact of the behaviour of each man on the aspirations of others. The rationally calculated, long-run optimum of each contributes to the long-run optimum of all.

Contrary to positive economics, sociology can be viewed as both an anti-utilitarian enterprise and a form of collectivised utilitarianism (Caillé, 1988). It is anti-utilitarian to the extent that, society being reducible neither to the political nor to the economic sphere, it introduces the holistic postulate that the whole is not reducible to the sum of its parts. This idea can be very easily identified in the work of Durkheim and of Marx, whose critique of political economy rests on the denial of an economic order which is independent of a social one. It is also more or less identifiable in Weber's work, for instance, in his distinction between the different types of social action. Despite the varying degree of commitment to holism and its consequences, sociologists have been united by the certainty that *Homo economicus,* the egoistic and calculating agent which pursues its interests or preferences, represents only a particular dimension of human action.

However, sociology is also committed to utilitarianism to the extent that authors like Marx and Durkheim were opposed not to utilitarianism itself, but to the idea that individuals were the atoms of social action. In this sense, their sociology also dealt with collective interests, be it through the Marxian notion of social class as a subject of history, or through Durkheim's idea of society as collective consciousness. It is in this sense that Caillé (1988) speaks of sociology as 'collective utilitarianism'.

Boudon, just like Caillé, believes that sociology does not represent a categorical refusal of the utilitarian paradigm. Rather, it refuses a strict application and definition of it. Differently from Caillé, Boudon believes that broad utilitarianism is in fact useful in sociology. For the latter, sociological attempts to do away with utilitarianism are either based on a misinterpretation of the general paradigm, or lead to very weak theories. In this sense, both Durkheim's and Parsons' critiques of utilitarianism (in particular their critique of Herbert Spencer) failed to grasp that utilitarianism was never presented as an atomist view according to which the anticipation of advantages was the only dimension of action. Spencer, to take only one example, never denied the influence of social mores in social action.[2] Boudon's main disagreement with the Parsonian refusal of utilitarianism is that utilitarianism was almost always presented as the equivalent of the modern notion of a model, i.e. it does not represent a realist image of the social actor (Boudon, 1989a). For him, Durkheim's and Parsons' critiques rest on utilitarianism as a 'conception of man', by which he means a realistic description of social actors, a critique which, he argues, he would endorse if it was really attributable to utilitarian thinkers.

For Boudon, utilitarianism can be generally conceived as a movement of reflection on the role of interests in social order and social change (Boudon and Bourricaud, 1982). Putting the problem in this way, instead of rejecting utilitarianism, most sociological theories tend to correct and complement it. In particular, and against a generalised utilitarianism, sociology has shown that:

1   There is no necessary harmony of interests or change of egoism into altruism. Harmony or conflict depends on the structure of the system of interdependence in which interests are expressed.
2   The interests of social actors are not interchangeable. They depend on the actors' positions in the social system, as well as on other complex contextual variables.
3   An actor may have conflicting interests.
4   There is a complex relation between values, beliefs and interests, therefore the last cannot always be taken for granted (Boudon and Bourricaud, 1982).

This means that the action paradigm, when applied to sociology, has to be based on a model of the actor which is more complex than the one normally presented by the *Homo economicus* of positive economic theories. Boudon's enterprise consists in developing a theory of rationality which, on the one hand, establishes the application limits of a rational-choice model based on a utilitarian perspective and, on the other, rejects those sociological theories which have an 'oversocialised view of man' as the result of an extreme anti-utilitarianism.[3] This enterprise assumes the form of the development of what Enzo Di Nuoscio (1996) calls a *'tertium genus'* between the irrational *Homo sociologicus* and the fully rational *Homo economicus* portrayed by strict forms of utilitarianism as applied to economics.

The notion of rationality thus assumes a very central role in the establishment of Boudon's sociology and, in particular, in the model of the actor which should account for the 'main causal mechanism' in the social domain. But what exactly does he understand by rationality? What status does the model of the rational actor assume in his theory? Does it represent some intrinsic feature of human agents, or is it merely a heuristic device which cannot be accessed in terms of its adequate description of reality? In order to understand this notion in Boudon's thought, as well as its status, it is necessary to understand his criticisms of the many definitions of rationality. As with the notions of theory, structure, causality, etc., the notion of rationality is also a polysemic one and its meaning is accessed through a critique of four distinct approaches, classified by him as the sceptical, the classical and utilitarian, the homonymic, and the Wittgensteinian (Boudon, 1995a).

The sceptical approach towards rationality

The sceptical approach consists in discarding altogether the problem of the definition of rationality by rendering the concept useless in sociology. According to this model, behaviour has to be explained by causes other than reasons. Although the distinction between causes and reasons is not absolute, since reasons are in effect a type of cause, some causes attributed to behaviour do not include the reasons for acting. The latter case is what is implied in Boudon's characterisation of the sceptical solution (Boudon, 1990a). This solution can be further divided in two variants: those which make recourse to affective causes and those which rely on non-affective causes. The former is also known as the Pascal–La Rochefoucauld model because it is summarised in La Rochefoucauld's notion that '*l'esprit est toujours la dupe du coeur*' (the mind is always duped by the heart), and in Pascal's idea that opinions are internalised either through understanding, or by will ('*les caprices téméraires de la volonté*' or the reckless whims of the will). In this sense, it is assumed that passions are almost always at the root of beliefs (Boudon, 1995a).

Although Boudon does not deny that affective factors can be sometimes legitimately invoked to explain actions and beliefs, he believes that this type of explanation is often used in cases where explanations by reasons appear to be more acceptable (Boudon, 1996a). Therefore, it is not a matter of rejecting explanations of the type 'She hit her son because she was angry', but one of recognising their fair share in social explanation and not taking them to be more general than they really are. In fact, it can be argued that what is at stake here is the level or the depth which explanation can assume. In certain contexts, I might be satisfied with an explanation of that sort, but that is certainly not a sociological level of explanation.

Models which rely on non-affective causes (which are also not reasons) can, in their turn, be exemplified through Lévy-Bruhl's theory of magic, where belief in magic is attributed to a primitive mentality which is fundamentally different from ours. According to this model, both logical and psychological mechanisms vary according to culture and society and, for this reason, they are fully attributed to social causes.

Both models assume that the *reasons* the subjects attribute to their beliefs/ actions are mere illusion and do not have any real consequences for the belief/action in question. Their difference lies in the fact that, whereas the former is based on a classical definition of irrationality, characterising actions of an impulsive or reflex type, the latter is based on a modern definition of irrationality which, according to Boudon, rests on the assumption that there are social or psychological causes which determine behaviour and these causes are not accessible. This difference assumes a major importance in Boudon's view to the extent that, whereas the former can be of some use in sociological analysis, the latter is rejected altogether:

> In the classical definition [of irrationality], the irrational behaviour (for instance, the impulsive behaviour inspired by anger) is both relatively conscious and transparent: I know that I have acted on anger and others can also perceive that. In this case, the irrational motivation is thus easily confirmed by both internal experience and external observation. It is completely different in the case of irrational behaviour in the modern sense: here, irrational motivation is a construct, inaccessible to internal experience and to external observation. Thus, the 'imitation instinct' (Tarde), 'mimetic desire' (R. Girard), 'resistance to change' (various authors), 'blindness by interest' (K. Marx), the 'unconscious drives' of the first Freud, 'false consciousness' (F. Mehring, F. Engels) can be neither experienced by the subject, nor observed, but only inferred. Such notions bring about serious methodological, psychological and sociological difficulties.
>
> (Boudon, 1986a: 295)[4]

Among the methodological objections to the 'modern' irrational model, Boudon argues, are that their theories are tautological and *ad hoc*. Lévy-Bruhl's theory of magic, for instance, is *ad hoc* to the extent that concepts like 'primitive mentality' or 'mystical explanation' were created with the sole intention of explaining the phenomena he wanted to explain. In other words, they have no legitimation other than supporting the causal relation that they try to establish. It is tautological because these notions do not really explain, but only paraphrase, magical phenomena (Boudon, 1990a).

Psychological objections refer to the existence of a hypothetical psychical apparatus which poses itself between consciousness and reality and imposes a deformed view of reality over the former. The problem with this idea (which is expressed through Marx's notion of the *camera obscura*, or Freud's initial definition of the unconscious) is that it postulates certain states that no human being has experienced. This does not mean that Boudon does not accept any definition of the unconscious: the social sciences admit its existence, but the concept cannot be turned into 'Pandora's box', nor can it be attributed causal efficiency (Boudon, 1986a: 304). According to Di Nuoscio (1996), Boudon believes that Freudian psychoanalysis does not imply any necessary deterministic relation between the unconscious and action, but there is a notion of the unconscious which limits itself to the description of subjective mental states in the pre-conscious phase.

Here it is worth showing that this descriptive account of the unconscious is in fact based on the same kind of argument that accounts for a nominalist or 'descriptive' conception of social structure. It is well known that, in his early writings, Freud stated a simple opposition between the unconscious and the pre-conscious/conscious. In this scheme, he located primitive instinctual wishes in the unconscious and attributed its remoteness from the other two to a censor which stands on the border between the unconscious and the pre-conscious. Although this model assumed that repressed elements could escape the censor and appear, for instance, in neurotic symptoms, thus having the possibility of being experienced by the subject or observed by an external observer, it did not explain how unconscious fantasies associated with neurotic symptoms could exhibit the same logical structure as those processes associated with the pre-conscious/conscious regions of the human *psyche*. This means that the attribution of certain contents to the unconscious was a somewhat speculative matter. This recognition made Freud abandon the model of the mind described primarily by its relationship to consciousness and adopt, instead, a model of the psyche composed of three agencies (the *id*, the *ego* and the *superego*) which were not sharply differentiated from the start. Their differentiation was a gradual process according to which the *ego* evolves from an interaction between the *id* and the external world, shades into the *id*, and then presents a dynamic unconscious component. The ego thus becomes responsible for (dynamic) unconscious activities such as fantasy formation and resistance (Goldberg, 1988), and these also present a causal influence on the conscious activities of the ego. This more dynamic model also makes access to the unconscious rather tentative and indirect; nonetheless, it introduces elements (lived experiences) through which some of its content can be accessed (or rather inferred), and not only postulated. But as with the former model, the main idea behind the notion of the unconscious is not of a descriptive, but of a causal nature; and this is in fact the only way in which any existence at all can be attributed to the unconscious. Here, as with the concept of social structure, it is only though its causal effects that one can infer the existence of a non-observable entity. It seems to me, though, that it is indeed unlikely that sociologists can base a theory of (social) action on psychological processes of that kind, especially when what is at stake is the determination of particular unconscious motives. But this certainly does not prevent us from acknowledging that there is more to action than what our (sociological) theories can account for. So much for Freudian models of the mind.

Among sociological objections to the 'modern' conception of irrationality presented by Boudon is the sociocentric perspective implied in an 'oversocialised view of man'. Naturally, he believes that some causal statements made in terms of the internalisation of norms and values are legitimate (Boudon, 1993e), but he makes the proviso that, when they are, they normally refer to a 'classical' definition of irrationality. On the other hand, such causal statements are not always sufficient to explain, for instance, why internalised norms remain operative. But here, once again, one can argue that what is at stake is the level of explanation which is required in each particular case, and it is important to recognise that no theory, be it psychological or sociological, can account for human action in its entirety. More to the point, it is only in this restricted sense that sociological theory can explain certain phenomena without reducing human action to its social dimension.

In a nutshell, the problem Boudon sees in the 'sceptical solution' is that it discards the very aim of social explanation. According to him, identifying the *reasons* for acting corresponds to the identification of *causes* in the natural world. Although Boudon believes, in a clearly Weberian fashion, that explanation through causes (other than reasons) is a 'necessary ingredient in the explanation of some behaviours' (Boudon, 1993e: 5), this is perceived as just an intermediate stage in the explanation of human affairs and is always insufficient when taken in isolation.

The classical and the utilitarian approaches and some attempts to correct them

The second solution to the problem of rationality is presented as two related ones: the classical and the utilitarian (Boudon, 1995a). Both are, in a sense, viewed as a kind of 'remedy' to the causal or sceptical solution, and constitute a very narrow definition of rationality. In this case, be it in classical economics or philosophy, rational action is defined as 'the set of actions or behaviours governed by objectively valid reasons' (Boudon, 1991b: 34). This view was shared by different authors such as Freud, Marx, Pareto, Bacon, Descartes, Pascal and Hume, and it is possible to find elements in their work according to which irrationality and illusion are but one thing, and to be rational is 'to see the world as it is and to adjust to it' (ibid.).

The classical solution consists in defining rationality by one of its forms: teleological or instrumental rationality. This form of rationality is characterised by the objectively valid adequacy of the means used to reach the end pursued by the subject. A particular contemporary case is the most standard form of rational-choice theory. Rational-choice theory is defined by Elster (1986:1) as a normative theory which 'tells us what to do in order to achieve our aims as well as possible. It does not tell us what our aims ought to be. ... Unlike moral theory, rational-choice theory offers conditional imperatives, pertaining to means rather than to ends.' It is sometimes supplemented by a theory of rational belief, which implies a correspondence between beliefs and the evidence available to the actor. Despite its variations, rational-choice theory rests on a classical definition of rationality, that is, 'the rationality of an action is ensured by its standing in the right kind of relation to the goals and beliefs of the agent' (ibid.).

Related to this classical definition (they normally go hand in hand) is the utilitarian solution to the problem of reason and rationality. According to a strict utilitarian notion of rationality, there should not only be an adequacy between means and ends, but the ends would have to be in accordance with the subjects' interests. In other words, it introduces the postulate of egoistic ends, be it in the classical notion of interest, or in the more contemporary notion of preference.

These two solutions constitute the domain of *Homo economicus* and, according to Boudon, a common objection to this approach is that it only explains the means, but not the end(s) of a given action. For Boudon, this objection misses the point for one main reason: it supposes that the subject evaluates first the ends, then the means, which is not always the case. In many cases, the evaluation of the ends depends on the evaluation of the means. In Boudon's own words, 'in many circumstances, action rests on the undecomposable evaluation of the whole constituted by ends and means and, since the evaluation of ends depends in this case on the evaluation of means, nothing prevents in principle that the evaluation of ends may be explained at least partially by the *Homo economicus* model' (Boudon, 1993e: 7).

It is not entirely clear what Boudon means by a partial explanation of ends. What is at stake here is not a discussion of the rationality or irrationality of ends, which is, in any case, irrelevant from a purely instrumental perspective. Boudon's argument implies that even a perfectly rational end, such as the pursuit of profit in capitalist societies, for instance, is not included as an aim (i.e. it does not even count as an end) if, for example, the means of attaining it presupposes something like my killing of every person who engages in the same sort of business as I do. The absurdity of this solution would prevent the consideration of this end in the sense that it is 'not worth being followed'. Considerations of this kind may justify the applicability of a moral dimension of utilitarianism, but it is not justified in some rational-choice approaches with a purely normative content. In the example above, the action is considered as not worth being followed because of its moral consequences, which have little to do with the instrumental aspects of the action. The obvious absurdity of the solution prevents the end from being considered only to the extent that there is a general moral code that is immediately understandable by every observer. In a purely normative sense, if the end does not exist as such, it does not have to be explained. If it does, a strict utilitarian perspective does not explain it, but merely takes its existence for granted. Of course there are cases in which the ends are considered to be so obvious that they do not require any explanation (thus justifying the applicability of this approach in such cases), but this does not mean that the model normally represented by *Homo economicus* can explain the ends, whether in a partial or in a deep manner.

Nonetheless, Boudon's argument is aimed at some sociological trends which presuppose that ends should be explained in an exclusively causal–

cultural fashion, and not at the idea that it is sometimes important to explain the origin of values and beliefs. For him, even when ends require explanation, it is sometimes possible to consider them as the effect of a rational calculus which is bounded by cultural factors. However, a 'bounded' rationality of this kind is not in the scope of a *Homo economicus* type of explanation.

This defence of the utilitarian perspective does not mean that Boudon accepts its generality. Its limited applicability is revealed by the fact that the utilitarian version rejects as irrational all actions which are not egoistically founded, presenting the additional problem of not being able to prove that altruism is always a form of egoism. Moreover, the reduction of rationality to its instrumental aspects, as in the classical definition of rationality, presents other kinds of problems, such as rejecting as irrational all actions whose adaptation of means to ends are problematic, as well as behaviour with no explicit aims (like beliefs, for instance).[5] Apart from defining actions which are not necessarily irrational as being so, some actions which do not follow the objectively valid means–ends adaptation are defined as such whenever the classical model is extended outside its scope.

Some types of actions which have no explicit aims are rendered irrational according to the narrow definition of rationality presented by both the classical and the utilitarian solutions. The problem with this view is that explaining some types of unintentional but meaningful behaviour is sometimes useful in the social sciences. Some reflex acts, for instance, may give us a clue to the types of values involved in certain groups. There are endless examples of unintentional but meaningful actions whose explanation may be important, such as when an observer who is particularly concerned about collective values sees a reaction of indignation when someone witnesses a thief stealing an old lady's bag (Boudon, 1993e). This indignation (supposing it was not meant to catch anyone's attention) was not aimed at any goals, but it is still both understandable and meaningful, particularly if one takes into account that the reaction is not only relative to the breach of one single value, such as stealing, but also to values such as respect for elderly people or not taking advantage of those who have some sort of disability, and so on. The reasons the observer had for behaving in that way are obviously not of an instrumental type. On the one hand, rational-choice theorists are right to exclude this kind of behaviour from their analyses, which are based on an instrumental rationality. On the other hand, this exclusion would not justify rendering such actions as irrational (in the sense that the actor had no reasons for performing them). The only element which may allow for the characterisation of such action as irrational is the narrow definition of rationality of the classical and utilitarian solutions: as intentional acts based on objectively valid reasons.

Boudon takes such cases to illustrate a type of rationality which is not goal-oriented, but value-oriented. It seems to me that the Weberian notion of affective behaviour would be better than the notion of *Wertrationalität* to describe the example in question, since the latter type of action implies the existence of a particular purpose, which is following a value.[6] If the feeling of indignation is not intended, then it cannot represent a deliberate intention of following a value. On the other hand, Boudon is right to stress its meaningful character, to include it as relevant in some types of explanation, and to point out that the rational-choice model would be inadequate to explain behaviour of this kind.

It is, however, important to consider that not all rational-choice theorists are naïve enough to postulate a generality of this model defined in terms of a restricted notion of rationality. Jon Elster (1989), for instance, argues that it has a limited scope and has to be complemented by something else (psychological, biological, sociological theories).

An opposite tendency is followed by Gary Becker, when, instead of limiting the scope of rational-choice theory, he extends the applicability of instrumental rationality by assuming stable sets of preferences (which means that tastes and preferences in general can be treated as mere data) and by extending the notion of the market to the sociological and psychological domains: 'all human behaviour can be viewed as involving participants who maximize their utility from a stable set of preferences and accumulate an optimal amount of information and other inputs in a variety of markets.' (Becker, 1986: 119). The use of the narrow notion of rationality is extended by the idea that, just as in a market situation, behaviour is guided by (hidden) objectively valid reasons. In this sense, Becker would characterise every death as a suicide, and the reason for this is that there is always a possible way of postponing one's own death which people choose not to follow. This could be 'confirmed' by some psychological theories through the existence of an alleged death wish (ibid.).

The tautological character of such a theory goes without saying. Postulating the existence of hidden objectively valid reasons allows Becker to attribute any choices to individuals, as long as they fit the means–end scheme of utilitarianism. The results of this postulate are twofold: either we attribute to the individual a choice that is not his or hers, or we interpret their choices in terms of a maximisation of utilities in purely tautological terms (Demeleunaere, 1994).

Given these problems that are present in the utilitarian and the classical definitions of rationality, Boudon's main contention with this narrow definition of rationality is that either it allows too much space for irrationality in human behaviour, and/or it leads to a theory that is not only abstract, but unrealistic, since it removes all cultural, social and psychological elements that give specificity to the individual. There is thus need for a more general theory of rationality that incorporates but also extends the narrow definition above.

There were some attempts to 'correct' the narrow definition of rationality proposed by the classical and the utilitarian approaches by assuming that the notion of optimisation or maximisation implicit in it is simply a regulative ideal, and that, in practice, it is often difficult or impossible to determine the best means to an end and the utility of the ends to be chosen. For Herbert Simon, for instance, individuals would choose not the best means to a given end, but only means which are 'satisficing'. Popper (1957), in his turn, insisted on the (methodological) importance of assuming that individuals act in an 'adequate' or 'appropriate' fashion, *vis-à-vis* a given situation. From there, he derives his notion of rationality. Braybrooke and Lindblom introduced the notion of *incrementalism* based on Hayekian and Popperian ideas about unintended consequences of action and on 'piecemeal engineering'. According to their incrementalism, rationality would consist in using strategies which guarantee a minimum risk, based on the gradual possibility of anticipating consequences (Boudon and Bourricaud, 1982).

The differences presented between these two groups of theorists is one of degree only, not one of essence. Despite the broader notion of rationality presented by the latter group, it is still based on an objective rationality, i.e. individuals choose the objectively best means (according to the state of knowledge, etc.) to attain their ends. The introduction of certain subjective states makes the notion of objectivity somewhat blurred, and the distinction between reality as it is and reality as it appears to subjects is not always accounted for, rendering the notion of rationality rather pointless. For instance, how would incrementalism deal with the problem of the short-term pleasure of smoking and the long-term risks involved in it? How can I rationally deny myself the pleasure of one cigarette which is based on minimum risk? How to rationally decide which is the moment to stop, even though I have the information that smoking is bad for my health from the start?

The Popperian notion of broad rationality is no less problematic. For Popper, the method of the social sciences should rely on the 'method of logic or rational construction', the 'zero method', which consists in assuming complete rationality on the part of the individuals concerned and estimating the deviation of the actual behaviour from this model. Its generality for the social sciences rests on the assumption that:

> ... in most social situations, if not in all, there is an element of *rationality*. Admittedly, human beings hardly ever act quite rationally (i.e. as they would if they could make the optimal use of all available information for the attainment of whatever ends they may have), but they act, none the less, more or less rationally.
>
> (Popper, 1957: 140)

The use of the zero method is therefore a means for grasping the rationality, the logic or the reasons behind a given action. According to Boudon (1991b: 36), this definition of the method of the social sciences as an instrument to identify reasons (as causes) of behaviour has led Popper, in some of his works, to accept the idea that 'any reason can be good provided it is perceived as such by the social actor'. For Boudon, the Popperian idea according to which any reason should be considered as causal is as difficult to accept as the idea that objectively invalid reasons are devoid of any causal power, as is implicitly assumed in the narrow definition. As Boudon (ibid.) elegantly writes in response to Popper, 'we all know that the fox of La Fontaine rejected the grapes not because they were sour, but because they were too high to be reached'.

In my view, though, one of the main problems with the Popperian notion of rationality refers to the ambiguous status of the rationality principle. On the one hand, it is considered to be a kind of covering law, a 'trivial general law' which allows for the generation of hypotheses on people's behaviour. In this sense, it represents an empirical assumption about human nature (Stokes, 1998). On the other hand, the principle is not falsifiable, which can only mean that it is not empirical but is truly a priori (which is clearly not the case, since Popper considers that actions can deviate from the pattern dictated by the model), or that, contrary to his falsification thesis, particular instances of empirical refutation are not sufficient for establishing the falsity of a law or of a scientific proposition. Either way, it implies a realist account of human nature, based on some intrinsic property of human beings. This solution, apart from going against Popper's 'anti-essentialistic' philosophy, is rejected by Boudon on the basis of the existence of both false and inconsistent beliefs, on the one hand, and, on the other, on the idea that rationality is not intrinsic to agents, but to actions.

A similar rejection of the narrow definition's assumption of objectively valid reasons as the only reasons bearing causal power is presented by H. Simon in his later works. Rationality is defined by him in a very broad sense: 'rationality denotes a style of behaviour that is appropriate to the achievement of given goals, within the limits imposed by certain conditions and constraints' (Simon *apud* Boudon, 1991b). This broad definition allows Simon to make a distinction between objective rationality, defined in terms of the classical solution, and subjective or bounded rationality. The important point for Boudon's own theory of rationality is that this distinction allows for the use of both a narrow and a broad definition of rationality, although it still presents some problems. Like Popper's, Simon's definition has the inconvenience of extending too much into the domain of rationality. The 'conditions and constraints' imposed on the individual may, according to Simon, be 'characteristics of the organism itself that it takes as fixed and not subject to its own control' (ibid.). In this sense, Boudon argues, a mad person whose identity is based on these characteristics is always subjectively rational, and this solution cannot be accepted.

Here it becomes clear that, for Boudon, the principle of rationality, be it in the narrow or in the broad definition, cannot be a true a priori notion, in the sense of representing an intrinsic feature of human agents, nor does it represent an empirical law, in the Humean sense of the term. Rather, it represents a model whose adequacy has to be empirically and theoretically established for each particular combination of action and situation. For this reason, the appeal of rational-choice models cannot, for Boudon, be attributed to the content of its principles (to maximise or, alternatively, to optimise the difference between costs and benefits), but to the fact that it explains actions through reasons. This means that theories based on the rational-choice model are able to identify an important causal mechanism which allows for the identification and explanation of many 'black boxes'. Their danger lies in its application in situations where they do not fit, for 'what is, in effect, a scientific explanation that does not aim at realism?' (Boudon, 1999a: 83).[7]

The homonymic definition of rationality

A third definition arises from what Boudon terms the 'homonymic solution', a terminology which could be easily translated into a nominalist account of rationality. According to him, this is the solution presented by authors like Agassi and Jarvie, Mario Bunge, and Habermas. These authors deal with the notion of rationality on irreducible and, to a certain extent, opposed levels and, in this sense, their relation is purely nominal (Boudon, 1995a). Jarvie and Agassi for instance, differentiate between rationality as applied to actions, meaning congruence between means and end, and rationality as applied to beliefs, meaning coherence within a belief system and/or coherence with reality or logical proof.

For Boudon (1993e), this distinction leads to a meaningless character-isation of action based on beliefs. This element of action, summarised by the statement 'X did Z because he/she believed T', cannot be said to be rational in any coherent way, since it presupposes two different notions of rationality which bear a nominal relation only. This distinction renders impossible the explanation of any action which is not purely instrumental, and, since Boudon believes this type of action is only a very limited case, the proposed homonymy is rendered useless:

> I do not see how a concept of rationality which cannot be clearly applied to the case where an action includes some belief can be at all useful, since, except in some cases of limited importance, action always includes beliefs. Either we discard actions including beliefs or we don't. If we don't, an action can only be qualified as rational in an unambiguous fashion under the condition that 'rational' has the same meaning when it is applied to actions as when it is applied to beliefs or more generally to *unpurposive* behaviours.
>
> (Boudon, 1993e: 9)

Habermas's distinction between communicative and instrumental rationality seems to rest on the same type of homonymy. Nonetheless, Boudon argues (1995a), a more attentive look into the Habermasian solution to the problem of the definition of rationality suffices to show that, although there is certainly some kind of discontinuity between the notions of communicative and instrumental rationality, their opposition cannot be purely nominal. This makes sense when one considers that the different types of rationality are the result of a historical process, based on the development of Reason, which can guarantee some basic common element between the two notions. On the other hand, Boudon (1991b) seems to suggest that Habermas' distinction is the result of his adoption of the Hegelian notion of Reason as a societal or holistic concept. Although it is impossible to imagine Habermas' theory in individualistic terms, Boudon maintains that Reason does not need to be treated in a purely holistic fashion. This critique of a holistic conception of Reason, seems, however, to be minimised in some of Boudon's later texts, where he tends to conceive of a general evolutionism when dealing with the 'irreversible' character of certain values, very much in accordance with the Weberian conception of history as rationalisation (see Boudon, 1999a).

The nominalist conception of rationality can also be attributed to Weber's distinction between purposive teleological and value-rationality, and it is probably the aforementioned connection between rationality and Reason that makes it possible to interpret Weber's notion of rationality as a homonymic concept.[8] For Boudon (1995a), however, Weber's concepts of rationality and rationalisation are used both in the individualistic and in the holistic mode. They may represent different notions, depending on whether they are applied to society as a whole or to individual action.

The homonymic solution is viewed by Boudon as resting on a false homonymy. Reason is a common element in different types of rationality, therefore they are not absolutely opposed. On the other hand, because the classical notion of Reason does not distinguish between its collectivist and individualist modes, it has to be used by Boudon in a very restricted manner, making it compatible with his methodology. This does not mean that he defines Reason in absolute terms. On the contrary, it is always considered as a social product, culturally and historically grounded, which has to be explained with recourse to specific social values.[9]

The Wittgensteinian conception of rationality

The fourth solution to the problem of defining rationality is termed 'Wittgensteinian', for it rests on Wittgenstein's distinction between two types of notions: those which bear transitive resemblance relations between objects described by 'non-polythetic' words, and those which bear intransitive (or not necessarily transitive) relations between objects described by 'polythetic' words. The term 'polythetic' is borrowed from the anthropologist R. Needham to account for those words whose meaning derives from the family resemblance which links their many uses (such as Wittgenstein's notion of 'game') (Boudon, 1990a). The idea behind the term polythetic is thus related to the meaning of words which cannot be strictly defined, because they always include and/or exclude particular properties, according to specific situations.

Non-polythetic words are exemplified by Boudon by the words 'armchair', 'chair', 'stool', which are all seating devices. The transitive character of their resemblance makes it possible to define them as non-polythetic words or words that can be defined in classical terms, i.e. by *genus proximum* and specific differences. Polythetic words, resting on the polythetic nature of intransitive objects, are illustrated by Boudon by the physical resemblance of related people: 'it may happen that the son resembles his mother, that the mother resembles her own mother, but that the grandson does not resemble his grandmother' (Boudon, 1995a: 535).[10] This sort of relation makes it impossible to strictly define certain concepts, insofar as the definition may include predicates which do not belong to the concept in question, and it may exclude certain predicates which are not common to all things designated by the concept. According to Boudon, this would be the case with concepts such as game, science, cause, paradigm, attitude, truth, etc., but this does not mean that they cannot refer to a *sui generis* reality.

Based on this distinction, Boudon classifies rationality as a polythetic term which has a well-defined relationship with the reality it describes, i.e. it describes a specific phenomenon which is real, and, although Boudon does not formulate the issue in these terms, it is real because it has real effects. In this sense, the set of actions which belong to the polythetic chain that defines rationality (that is, the family resemblances which give meaning to the concept) should take the form 'X had reasons to do or to believe Y, since ...'. This general form is opposed to an explanation in irrational terms, which, for Boudon (1995a: 541), takes the form 'X did not have reasons to believe or to do Y, but ...'.[11] This solution would, according to him, allow for a clear distinction between rationality and irrationality, showing, at the same time, that it depends on a complex number of variables and cannot rest on a general a priori distinction. As a corollary, Boudon argues that there is no priority regarding rational or irrational explanations: everything depends on the action and the social phenomenon in question. Being dependent on the type of action, rationality cannot be taken as a basic defining feature of human nature. It is nonsensical to make use of presuppositions such as 'people are rational' or 'people are irrational'. Rationality and irrationality are predicates which apply to behaviour, actions, beliefs, not to people in general and, for this reason, 'the social sciences can dispense with the idea of answering these naïve ontological questions. What is true is that *certain* behaviour, *certain* actions and *certain* beliefs can be explained in a rational fashion, and others, in an irrational one' (ibid.: 547).[12]

In an important sense, however, Boudon's notion of rationality can be compared to the Marxian notion of labour being intrinsic to the human nature: it does not point to a human essence which is asocial and ahistorical, but to certain tendencies and capabilities which are socially acquired and only exercised under the appropriate conditions. This comparison shows that, contrary to Boudon's claims, treating rationality as intrinsic to agents can be useful to the extent that the concept allows for the consideration of a basic human property which characterises human beings as a particular type of agent. It is only in this way that Boudon's notion of rationality can overcome the ambiguous status of Popper's principle of rationality.

It is thus no accident that Boudon is particularly concerned with establishing a more 'realistic' model of the actor than the one presented by rational-choice theories. This realistic model would have to consider the variability of actions and beliefs and thus go beyond the alternatives represented by *Homo economicus* and *Homo sociologicus*. Since the latter is based on a strict notion of rationality (this is one of the reasons why *Homo sociologicus* is taken to be irrational), the new model has to rest on a broad notion of rationality which does not allow for a stipulatory definition, but only for a semantic one, theoretically based. Moreover, this broad notion of rationality has to recognise the place of irrationality in human behaviour.

The rational model in the broad sense: towards a synthetic theory of rationality

Convinced of the impossibility of defining rationality in strict terms, Boudon rejects all classical and modern definitions and argues (1991b) that it was Max Weber who came the closest to doing it in a satisfactory way. First, Weber assumes that understanding means, in most cases, retrieving the actor's reason for behaviour.[13] Second, he recognises that there are some cases in which no reasons can be invoked to explain an action, as in the case of some affective actions. Third, Weber admits a difference between the reasons which the actor attributes to his/her actions, and the reasons which had a real causal influence, i.e. he admits the possibility of reasons having only a covering up function. But since reasons can also have a causal affect without being objectively valid, this does not mean that Weber subscribes to the Paretian postulate that non-objective reasons have merely a covering up function.

These traits which are found in Weber's work lead Boudon to conclude that Weber accounts for all the possible situations dealt with by different accounts of rationality: situations where reasons are objectively valid and have a causal effect on behaviour; situations where reasons are only subjectively grounded and have a causal effect; situations where reasons do not have a causal effect and have a covering up function (Boudon, 1991a: 39). This amounts to saying that Weber's notion of rationality rests on the distinction between objective and subjective reasons, and that the latter can be interpreted in terms of good reasons because, although they are objectively invalid, they are not arbitrary.

This definition, together with H. Simon's distinction between objective and subjective rationality, is thus the starting point of Boudon's synthetic theory of rationality. Notwithstanding that, Boudon tries to overcome the problem he identified in Simon's subjective rationality: it gives too much space for rationality, for instance, by regarding behaviours such as madness or fanaticism as rational. The way he proposes to get out of this dilemma is to identify rationality with all the *good* or *strong reasons* the individual has for acting in a certain way, a solution which, he believes, is implicit in Weber's notion of value-rationality. Contrary to Weber, however, Boudon does not assume the conflict between value and instrumental rationality in the same way that Weber does. According to Weber (1978: 26):

> Value-rational action may ... have various different relations to the instrumentally rational action. From the latter point of view, however, value-rationality is always irrational. Indeed, the more the value to which action is oriented is elevated to the status of an absolute value, the more 'irrational' in this sense the corresponding action.

The relative irrationality of value-rationality is, according to Demeleunaere (1994: 262), based on two heterogeneous aspects. On the one hand it may refer to the irrationality of values itself; on the other hand, it refers to the carefree character of value-rationality in relation to its means and subsidiary consequences. The first of these aspects leads Weber to the pessimistic conclusion that it is impossible to (rationally) decide between two systems of values. Between the Nietzschean pessimistic conclusion and the Kantian rationalism inspiring Weber's theory of knowledge, Boudon opts for the second:

> We can ... easily conclude that 'disenchantment' – in the sense of the disappearance of the belief on transcendence – inevitably leads to a polytheistic anarchy of values: if values do not have an exterior reality, they are not values; or, the extinction of transcendence is strictly linked to the extinction of values; the extinction of transcendence thus implies the extinction of values. But this syllogism does not distinguish in reality the modalities of values' representation and values themselves.
>
> (Boudon, 1995a: 294)[14]

In this sense, Boudon believes that the Weberian theme of the disenchantment of the world is not incompatible with his notion of value-rationality. There is no reason why the first process should lead to contemporary values not being established on a solid basis. Only this basis cannot be accounted for in terms of a narrow view of rationality. The irreversible character of the disenchantment of the world comes from the fact that mythical explanations are more and more replaced by theories which rest on plausible and 'light' theses. But this does not prevent the same process in terms of values. Moreover, the heuristic value of Weber's notion of value-rationality lies in the fact that it extends rationality beyond the realm of the narrow definitions given by the utilitarian and the classical traditions, thus allowing for the possibility of explaining the origin of beliefs and world views.

For Boudon (1991b: 39), despite the differences between axiological and teleological rationality, Weber did not necessarily use the notion of rationality in two different senses. There is an implicit definition of rationality which makes it possible to include Weber in the list of philosophers such as Kant, Ryle or Wittgenstein, according to whom it is possible to safely apply a distinction without being able to define it (i.e. 'to associate criteria with the distinction' in the way that polythetic terms require). In this sense, Weber's implicit notion of rationality also anticipates H. Simon's subjective rationality to the extent that it:

> ... proposes to treat a piece of behaviour as rational under the condition that we are able to provide for the behaviour an explanation of this type: 'the actor behaved in the way he behaved because he had good reasons to do so, namely...', where the notion of good reasons indicates that the reasons of the actor can be objectively invalid. Still, these reasons should not be arbitrary. On the contrary, any observer should be convinced that in the same circumstances, if he would have been in the same position as the actor, he would possibly have done the same thing. Thus, the reasons of the actor must have a universal validity.
>
> (Boudon, 1991b: 38)

The advantages of adopting a broader notion of rationality in social explanation is illustrated by an imaginary dialogue between David Hume and Anthony Downs (Boudon, 1989c; Boudon, 1990a). In his *Essays: Moral, Political and Literary*, Hume argues that political parties bring people together according to three mechanisms: interests, solidarity and principles. The first mechanism refers to the idea that people affiliate within a given party because they have common interests. The second mechanism attributes affiliation to the fact that people can protect their sense of 'belonging' to a social group; affiliation to political parties would, in other words, protect people's collective identity of groups already in existence. The third mechanism attributes the existence of political parties to ideas or principles.

The idea that some political parties are grounded on principles (especially abstract speculative principles) is a puzzling one for Hume. According to Boudon, the strangeness this idea generates in Hume is because he has a narrow definition of rationality in mind. According to the narrow definition (especially as presented by the consequentialist version of utilitarianism), the only rational way of endorsing a political party would be by determining the outcomes of the programme and checking whether they are acceptable or not. This mechanism is reversed in affiliation according to principle: 'instead of checking whether the consequences of a political program are good or not, the voters wonder whether it is grounded on the right principles' (Boudon, 1989c: 178). This reversal leads Hume to offer an 'irrational' explanation for this behaviour, but, Boudon argues, Hume regards this solution as a kind of paradox.

The paradox was solved by Downs in *An Economic Theory of Democracy*, when he showed that choosing between two political programmes is not rational in the narrow sense for three main reasons: first, it is very difficult, if not impossible, to determine with certainty the outcomes of the two programmes; second, one has no certainty whether the programme will be applied in the way it was presented; finally, even if voters could overcome the first two difficulties, they might still not know which programme is better for them. In any of these cases, evaluating the principles on which the programme rests might be a good alternative. This evaluation is, for Downs, made in terms of ideology: the rational voter is ideological. According to Boudon (ibid.), the choice of this term shows that, although Downs's solution contributed to diminishing the influence of the narrow view of rationality, he was still dominated by it.

It is not difficult to realise why Boudon attributes a narrow conception of rationality to Downs' theory: the theory of ideology which lies behind it presupposes a theory of motivation based on passions or emotions, i.e. it does not take ideology to be based on good reasons. Boudon tries to substitute the explanation of cognitive biases based on affective mechanisms for an explanation based on intellectual ones (Bouvier, 1997). For this reason, Boudon argues that Downs's lesson would be expressed better by the idea that 'voters try to meet the situation they are faced with through the help of reasonable conjectures or theories, for instance, the conjecture that a program grounded on certain principles will likely lead to consequences congruent with these principles.' (Boudon, 1989c: 179). In other words, the reasons of individuals can be grounded on good reasons which, despite their false character, can still be said to be subjectively good.

The importance of this imaginary discussion between Hume and Downs rests mainly on the fact that, as soon as a broader notion of rationality is adopted, some types of behaviour that are taken to be mysterious or incomprehensible become more easily understandable. Apart from that, it shows that the good reasons the actors have to do what they do 'have the status of conjectures, principles or theories that most people with the same level of information and/or interest in the question they are confronted with would endorse' (ibid.: 180), and this points to the hermeneutical or pre-interpreted character of social life.

It becomes clear that the model of actor that Boudon adopts is indeed very cognitively oriented, sharply contrasting with those models according to which desires have some sort of priority over beliefs in motivational terms. This model of actor has deep consequences not only for Boudon's theory of knowledge, but also for his theory of morals: the adhesion to moral principles is triggered by a belief in what is right, not by sentiment, which is desire-related (Hollis, 1987: 68–9). This does not mean denying the affective dimension of human morality:

> [T]he sentiments of justice or injustice, legitimacy or illegitimacy are rightly so called since they include an affective dimension: nothing is

more painful than injustice. However, they are, at the same time, grounded on reasons. Moreover, the strength of the sentiments is proportional to the strength of the reasons: I suffer more from injustice if I am convinced of the validity of my rights.

(Boudon, 1997a: 21)

In this way, Boudon establishes a notion of rationality that not only accounts for the rationality of action, when it is rational, but explains why people believe in certain ideas or follow certain moral principles: they are grounded on reasons which can be shown to be strong for the situation in question. The main point of the theory of subjective rationality is that, following Weber, it distinguishes between grounded and objective validity by implying that cognitive rationality is the 'product of the discordance between the complexity of the world and the cognitive capacities of the subject' (Boudon, 1992a: 6).

Subjective or contextual rationality, contrary to the rational-choice model, accounts for all those cases in which it is possible to explain behaviour according to the semantic definition: 'X had good reasons to do Y, since he/she believed Z', and Z can be shown to be meaningful, in the sense that it is true, plausible, reasonable, adequate to a given situation, etc. In this way, the narrow definition of rationality becomes a particular case of subjective rationality, namely when the belief in question is true. The difference between them lies in the fact that, whereas the first type of belief can be validated by an operation of confrontation with the real world, the second type includes those beliefs which cannot be and are actually not validated by this operation (i.e. ideas which are shown to be false). This idea was developed in Chapter 2, both in Boudon's theory of ideology and in his characterisation of Simmel effects. I will refrain from repeating myself here.

The difference between positive and normative beliefs is that, in the explanation of the latter, Z is not shown to be true or plausible, but good, fair, legitimate, etc. In this sense, believing in Z can also be shown to rest on good reasons, provided one understands 'reason' here in a very broad sense, i.e. as making sense, as presenting a meaning for the actor. At the same time that Boudon extends his analysis to normative beliefs, he proposes a substitution of the notion of subjective rationality for that of cognitive rationality.[15]

Boudon's notion of cognitive rationality leads to a cognitivist theory of values that rests on six theses (Boudon, 1995a):

1   Value and moral judgements do not rest on a different basis from assertoric judgements. Judgements concerning what the world should be like are no different, in terms of their justification, from those concerning what the world is like. Moral convictions are experienced as such by individuals inasmuch as they rest on the feeling that they are justifiable by a system of strong reasons which can be communicated.

2   The only way of judging a proposition is by examining the reasons on which it is based and by determining its solidity.
3   Arguments may vary according to their degree of validity.
4   Factual judgements and value judgements are often combined and interpenetrated. This is particularly the case when one is dealing with consequentialist criteria: 'X is bad because its application produces consequences which everybody will think are hateful'. And the fact that everybody finds its consequences hateful is a factual judgement. Of course this reduction of value judgements into factual judgements does not always happen, but it represents an important case. There are also analytic criteria for accessing the validity of value judgements. This is the case when we argue that democracy is a good thing. And it is good because the main principles on which it rests derive from the notion of good government.
5   A good argumentation (in both assertoric and axiological domains) is a set of propositions where each one is acceptable.
6   There is no unique theory made up of a finite number of propositions allowing the deduction of all true and false statements about reality. In the same way, there is no single system of propositions allowing for the deduction of all just and unjust statements.

These theses clearly show that the element that allows Boudon to speak of a cognitive rationality in his theory of values is their objective character. But this objectivity assumes a special meaning, which I shall try to show here. It should not be taken in the sense of a strict conformity with reality because of his conception of science as a fallible enterprise, but in terms of a socially constructed truth which is, at the same time, more or less compatible with reality. For Boudon (1995a), there is not one arithmetic, biological or medical truth, but rather various arithmetic, biological and medical truths which are linked by different theories. The socially constructed character of truth is evident even in those areas of knowledge which are taken to be purely objective. Consider the following example taken from mathematics (ibid.: 333): why is a proposition such as 'there is no whole p and q such that $p/q = \sqrt{2}$' objectively valid? Because this proposition is correctly deduced from principles according to the rules of logical deduction. Because 'correctly' refers to these rules of logical deduction, it is, in a sense, a constructed truth. Moreover, given the impossibility of making an *ad infinitum* regression of all its principles, one normally accepts some of these principles as true. Although it would be possible in principle to have arithmetic based on other principles, the existing ones explain reality in a satisficing way, and the consensus established over their truth is the product of solid reasons. Not that consensus is a proof of truth, but 'when consensus appears, it has to be explained by making it the product of reasons likely to be perceived as objectively strong' (Boudon, 1997a: 13).

    Although axiological propositions do not rest on a finite system of axioms like the one defining arithmetic truths, their validity is also accessed through the solidity of reasons which are at their basis. The variability of collective feelings over a question such as the value of different political systems is regarded by Boudon more as a matter of individuals being in different cognitive environments than of a lack of objectivity over those values. According to him, history affects the discovery of truth, not truth itself. In this sense, the history of moral theory should not be taken as proof that moral values lack objectivity, but only as evidence that the theories about them are a social product. As a social product, theories about moral values are affected in a twofold way: not only does the cognitive environment change, but so does the broader social situation to which they refer. In this sense, value judgements are context related, but they present a universal kernel which allows for a certain degree of objectivity.

The contextual character of value judgements cannot be opposed to objectivity or universality. Relativism and scepticism are not compatible with cognitive rationality. Cognitive rationality springs from an interactionist conception which tries to overcome the opposition between universalism and relativism. For Boudon (1995a), there is an organic relation between the universal and the singular according to which the variability of value judgements does not lead to the conclusion that universals are the product of illusion. This organic relation is revealed in his interactionist analysis: when one knows the structure of a system of interaction, one can normally deduce the feelings of justice or injustice which will be produced in the individuals placed in that context. Feelings of justice or injustice 'translate' the reasons that the actors do or do not have for endorsing the system of interaction in question. The universal element of this type of analysis rests on the assumption, well established in the contractualist tradition, that what is perceived as just or unjust will be perceived as such by any individual. This is, for Boudon, the basic condition of *Verstehen*. On the other hand, and this is an element which is normally overlooked in the aforementioned tradition, little or nothing can be said about this perception if one does not take into account the data which were present (and, in a sense, also created) in the actors' minds. And this is the singular, contextual element of the analysis.

The principle of equality of contribution–retribution, for instance, is a universal one, analytically deducible from the notion of social exchange. In this sense, it points to non-consequential reasons for its adoption. On the other hand, social actors know that there are some particular conditions which must be fulfilled in order for this principle to be applied. They know, for instance, that contributions and retributions have to be commensurable. When they are not, actors operate what they regard as an acceptable synthesis between the principles of justice in question and the cognitive complexity which they face. This synthesis, which constitutes the core of the notion of cognitive rationality, renders a formalist solution to the problem of justice impossible.[16]

The combination of universal and contextual elements in the model of cognitive rationality makes Boudon argue for a particular kind of relativism which, according to him, should not entail the lack of objectivity of the model's conclusions. This is what he terms 'Kantian relativism', i.e. 'the theory according to which knowledge is possible only thanks to a priori notions' (Boudon, 1990b: 229). But these a priori notions are not absolute in the sense that Kant proposed, but based on shared knowledge which is present in the minds of individuals.

This has an important consequence for Boudon's theory of morals. Although, like Kant's metaphysics of morals, it is based on rational principles, rationality can be defined not in absolute universal terms, but in contextual ones. Although both theories are basically anti-consequentialist, Kant's anti-consequentialism rests on the impossibility of defining 'good' in empirical terms. Good reasons, on the other hand, are intrinsically related to empirical conditions.

According to Kant (1990), moral laws are universal because they rest on a general rule (the categorical imperative) which tells us which maxims or axioms are relevant for making a moral decision.[17] This rule is a priori, because it does not depend on any particular context to be arrived at. On the contrary, it depends solely on the concepts of pure reason.[18] Actions can have genuine moral worth if they are based on good will, which is a category deriving from freedom and Reason. Good will is the only thing in the world which can be conceived as good without any qualification, hence the anti-consequentialist conclusion: 'the good will is not good because of what it effects or accomplishes or because of its competence to achieve some intended end; it is good because of its willing (i.e. it is good in itself)' (ibid.: 10).

Good will is autonomous because it is not dependent on Nature's laws; rather, it is the result of people's reason (i.e. their ability to think correctly), which allows them to think of themselves as free entities, with free will. People are, in a sense, above Nature: they do not work according to laws, but based on conceptions of laws, i.e. according to principles (ibid.: 29). But in order that these principles are freed from their contextual character, they must refer to an imperative of an objective law of reason, conceived as a principle of reason which holds for everyone, independently of a will which is subjectively determined by things other than this general law. Reason is, therefore, the universal kernel which prevents relativism.

Kant is, nonetheless, rather sceptical about human rational competence: 'man is affected by so many inclinations that, though he is capable of the Idea of a practical pure reason, he is not so easily able to make it concretely effective in the conduct of his life' (ibid.: 5). In this sense, morals are subject to all kinds of corruption, and a moral action may be purely contingent or spurious if it is performed merely *in conformity to* the moral law. In order for it to be genuinely moral, it must be performed *for the sake of* the law. Only actions performed for the sake of the moral law, i.e. according to the categorical imperative, can be rendered objectively moral. Maxims which orient people's actions must be distinguished from that objective principle, because it contains 'the practical rule which reason determines according to the conditions of the subject (often his ignorance or inclinations) and is thus the principle according to which the subject acts.' (Kant, 1990: 37). The latter are not categorical imperatives, but hypothetical imperatives.

Good reasons are, by definition, reasons which are context related, and in this sense they refer to practical rules, not to moral laws. Because no definition of 'good', other than that of good will, is considered by Kant as truly analytical; no conception of 'good government', for instance, could objectively ground a moral conception of justice. Whereas Kant's notion of a priori refers to judgements that are necessary and universal, Boudon's a priori judgements are neither necessary nor universal. Of course they are not completely contingent (in the sense of arbitrary), but refer to a framework which is necessarily contextual. Objectivity must be understood in a very specific sense because '... no "fact" is "neutral"; it is *theory-* as well as *question-laden*' (Boudon, 1990b: 235).

The core of Boudon's argument on the objectivity of moral judgements is that the historical character of the axiological domain should not lead to any conclusions about its lack of objectivity. Normative rules change, as do rules relating to other (descriptive) domains. Both in science and in morality, questions may be provisionally unsolved, and some may never be solved, but this does not mean that some are not solved or provisionally solved (at least until new questions emerge) (Boudon, 1997a). Changes in moral rules are related to one condition: that the present state of affairs is perceived as unsatisfactory, i.e. that the real can be judged with the aid of the ideal (Boudon, 1995a: 372), and this ideal is not always the result of a given framework, but can be the result of their rejection. Theories which deal merely with the adaptive function of values, such as functionalist or consequentialist rational-choice theories, tend to overlook this fact and implicitly assume that the real is good. Incidentally, only this assumption would guarantee the reduction of axiological to instrumental rationality.

The possibility of objectively grounding moral values rests, contrary to some of Boudon's own statements, on a conception of rationality as 'a fundamental trait of human nature. As a consequence, an idea which is superior to another from the rational point of view is itself furnished with an intrinsic force' (Boudon, 1999a: 78).[19] In this sense, 'rationality has priority over irrationality in that irrationality can only occur as a defect in a rational being' (Collier, 1999: 106). This 'intrinsic force' of rational ideas thus comes from the very possibility of grounding them on reality: the principles guiding moral life can, like any other principles, be assessed in terms of their truth or falsity. The difference between moral and scientific ideas does not rest on the former's lack of cognitive grounding, but simply on the fact that, whereas scientific ideas are produced in an environment which is subject to widely accepted rules, moral or practical ideas are cast in the public sphere, where consensus is always harder to achieve (Boudon, 1999a).

Now that the real can be good or bad implies that there is objectivity in values, that values are intrinsic to facts or that moral discourse is about something 'which exists independently of us and can be discovered by us' (Collier, 1998: 695). This, in its turn, implies that, although there is a place for universalisation in morals, contrary to Kant's abstract universalism, it must be grounded in reality, in concrete cases or, in Collier's words (ibid.: 699), in 'some more or less universal reality mediating the particular desire and the universal project of emancipation'. Only, according to Boudon, establishing the objectivity of this reality is always a problematic issue insofar as this is always done on the basis of models, theories, etc., whose adequacy can never be fully established given his anti-realist presuppositions. Problems of objectivity of knowledge will be addressed in Chapter 4, although it is worth pointing out here that the possibility of objectively grounding morality rests on the possibility of objectively grounding reality's intrinsic worth, and this presupposes realist descriptions of reality.

Such realistic descriptions of values does not, once again, imply essentialism. The possibility of establishing objective moral judgements does not rest on a conception of values as a Platonic entity, as a separate order which is distinct from Nature and society. According to Collier (1999: 58), such a view would require 'some kind of supernatural moral sense with which to recognise the values'. The existence of such a sense can be denied, given the actual diversity of moral values. Contrary to a Platonic perspective, values inhere in things that compose this world, and 'since worth inheres in real beings, a change in the beings that there are changes the values that there are' (ibid.: 59). This means that communitarianism is essentially correct to stress the contextual character of values, but it errs in replacing the abstract Cartesian moral subject by a collective subject which assumes the features of human persons and, consequently, in denying the constraint of forces outside the social structure. Like Boudon, critical realists also reject the holism inherent in certain kinds of communitarianism, for society and culture cannot be considered as supraindividual entities:

> Society is neither a bundle of separate individuals nor is it a collective subject or suprapersonal organism. It is a set of relations between individuals and their environment, relations which pre-exist any given individual, and partly constitute the character and the powers of the related individuals. Society exists: it is not a mere plural of 'person' ...; but societies (plural) do not exist – nor does a Society (singular); 'society is not a count-noun. Society is an open textured structure, without boundaries or corporate identity.
>
> (Collier, 1999: 60)

This essentially means that not only is the objective value of things partly independent of society, but so also are the human powers to correctly access these values. The relative independence of human persons from their social environment cannot, however, be interpreted as them standing in some Archimedean standpoint which grants them clairvoyance. As Boudon has demonstrated through his notion of cognitive rationality, cognitive ideas can be true or false, but their discovery is part of a historical process which is always contingent. There is, in this sense, a pragmatic dimension to human knowledge. But contrary to the pragmatism of James and Dewey, which tends to reduce truth to usefulness, the pragmatic dimension of knowledge is related to James Pierce's idea according to which truth is a regulative ideal and is always guided by certain cognitive interests (Boudon, 1999a). For this reason:

> … we have to recognize that there is an inherent ambiguity or bipolarity in our use of terms like 'causes', 'laws', 'facts' (and even 'truths') and to be prepared, whenever necessary, to disambiguate them, distinguishing the transitive (social or making) from the intransitive (ontological or finding) employment of these terms.
>
> (Bhaskar, 1991: 10)

It is the implicit realisation of such a need that leads Boudon to define rationality as a polythetic word which, despite having its meaning defined by its relations to other words, cannot be reduced to a mere language game. In a clear opposition to structuralists and post-structuralists, Boudon does not perceive language as self-referential. Rather, the meaning of rationality refers to a well-established relation between cognitive ideas and the reality to which they refer. This means that it can only be defined in an argumentative fashion which assumes the form: 'X did Z because he/she had good reasons for doing/believing Z, since …'. The types of argument after the dots can be made more or less complex, depending on the type of phenomenon to be explained and on the questions the researcher wants to answer. Examples of different types of arguments, which could be indefinitely developed, are given by Boudon (1993e: 17):

> … (1) since Z was the best way of reaching G,
> … (2) since X believed Z was the best way of reaching G and that he had good reasons for believing it, since …
> … (2.1) Z is true,
> … (2.2) Z is a consequence of T and that X had good reasons for believing T, since …
> … (2.3) Z is good,
> … (2.3.1) since it is desirable to all,
> … (2.3.2) since it results from T,
> … (2.3.2.1) and that X had good reasons for believing T,
> … (2.3.2.1.1) since…

Concluding remarks

In this chapter I have tried to show how Boudon develops a theory of rationality in order to deal with the second principle of the action paradigm: explaining social phenomena means retrieving the meaning of the individual actions which are their basis. This principle rests on the Weber–Popper postulate that individuals always act more or less rationally and, in this sense, the meaning of an action often rests on the reasons the actors have for acting. This 'rationalistic' (in the weak sense of rationalism as defined by Hollis; see Chapter 1, Endnote 8) conception of human nature rules out a common sociological model which defines *Homo sociologicus* as a mere recipient of social norms and values, and brings it closer to its utilitarian cousin, *Homo economicus* (in particular, to a conception of *Homo economicus* whose motivation is not primarily dictated by passions, but by intellect).

Despite the heuristic value of *Homo economicus* to social explanation, sociology has shown that it can only account for a limited number of social phenomena. The solution to this problem is presented by Boudon through a redefinition of the notion of rationality according to which human behaviour is neither purely instrumental nor socially determined (although it is socially grounded).

This theory of rationality, which defines rationality in terms of the good reasons individuals have for acting in a given context or situation, is considered by Boudon to present a number of advantages over the models of *Homo economicus* and *Homo sociologicus* which are established on a narrow definition of rationality. First, it guarantees the place of irrationality in human behaviour without assuming that actors are always, or mostly, irrational. Second, it recognises that instrumental rationality is a particular case that is not always pertinent. Third, it allows for the explanation of a number of non-purposeful behaviours which are at the root of purposeful actions. Last, but not least, it reconciles sociology and economics by establishing a more realistic model than the ones presented by the major traditions of these disciplines.

One particular problem seems to arise from Boudon's characterisation of the social actor and is strictly linked to the rationality principle which derives from it. One the one hand, it is clear that Boudon is trying to avoid the unrealistic presuppositions of a rational, in the strict sense, model of actor. Rationality is conceived as not being intrinsic to agents, but as contingently applying to actions or beliefs. It is a possible, though not necessary, outcome of the use of reason under particular circumstances. Given this, he believes, no model of actor can be conceived in terms of its intrinsic properties or powers. This bears direct consequences for the centrality attributed to the notion of rationality to the extent that the status of the rationality principle is ambiguous: in some cases rationality is conceived as being a model which does not refer to any intrinsic properties of agents; in others, it is considered as an a priori truth, in the sense that it represents an essential anthropological trait.

This problem can, once again, be resolved within a naturalist–realist framework. According to this framework, 'agents are defined in terms of their tendencies and powers, among which in the case of human agents, are their reasons for acting' (Bhaskar, 1979: 118). Reasons, in their turn, are conceived, in a way not very distant from Boudon's, as 'beliefs rooted in the practical interests of life'; and a person's essence, in terms of 'what he is most fundamentally disposed to do (or become): that set of effective beliefs that determines his psychic (and behavioural) identity, and fixes him in his particularity as a kind' (ibid.: 123). These dispositions or tendencies, as in any law of Nature, are only exercised given the appropriate conditions, and it is contingent that these conditions are met. In this sense, the only difference between human action and the natural order is that the former is caused by states of mind, but since these states of mind are as real as any other causes, this allows Bhaskar (ibid.) to formulate the principle that 'for every action (or belief) there is a set of real reasons, constituting its rationale, which explains it'. In this sense, the centrality accorded to explanation through reasons does not rest on the fact that, more often than not, individuals act rationally, for this is only a consequence of the actualisation of certain powers under particular conditions. This is, in my view, more in accordance with the notion of cognitive rationality and provides a particularly powerful justification for the superiority of rational moral values over irrational ones: they represent the actualisation of a fundamental human capacity whose absence is (normally) related to particular social conditions.

Apart from the characterisation of the social actor, the theory of cognitive rationality expounded in this chapter also deals with the establishment of the causal chains between the social structure, beliefs and actions. The reasons which are considered as bearing a causal effect on action are selected, in Boudon's theory, according to the *Verstehen* process, an indispensable element in his sociology of action. According to the main thesis of the theory of cognitive rationality, the meaning of actions and beliefs is understandable when they rest on good reasons, and reasons are good when they rest on plausible conjectures (Boudon, 1993e). Now, as we have seen, 'plausible conjectures' are taken to be a social product and, as such, both the understanding of actions based on these conjectures and the explanation of social phenomena based on these actions have to distinguish between beliefs based on good reasons, and objectively valid knowledge, whose conjectures are not only plausible, but true. This, in its turn, presupposes both the possibility of using the agents' own understanding of their situation in order to reconstruct the causal chain of events, and of checking the validity of that understanding by establishing which reasons were effective. This problem is strictly linked to the nature of social explanation and its relation to understanding and interpretation. This constitutes the subject of Chapter 4.

4 Understanding, explanation and objectivity

The Italian methodologist Enzo Di Nuoscio defines the aim of actionist sociologies as the reconstruction of the links between reason, action and social phenomena. The first of these links is tackled through the notion of understanding; the second, through that of explanation (Di Nuoscio, 1996: 83). In this chapter, I shall investigate the meaning of these two notions in Boudon's work, as well as their relations. The importance of this procedure lies in establishing the possibility of an objective account of social reality based on his paradigm of social action and, in particular, on his theory of cognitive rationality. I shall start this investigation by examining the way in which Boudon classifies recent sociological theories and their commitment to understanding and explanation. This will allow me to situate his approach within sociological theory better, providing a basis for determining its specific traits.

Boudon (1983) classifies contemporary social theory in terms of three main paradigms: the neo-Durkheimian, the interpretative and the neo-Weberian. According to him, these paradigms are hardly compatible, but represent different useful approaches to social research, depending on its aims, as well as on the data which are available. However, he suggests that the neo-Weberian paradigm is the most fertile of them all, because it conforms to two important epistemological principles: first, it denies that the social sciences can establish empirical regularities with universal validity; second, it postulates that these sciences must, like the natural sciences, submit to the procedure of rational critique.

The neo-Durkheimian paradigm

The theories which make up the neo-Durkheimian paradigm have in common the fact that their main (if not sole) aim is the discovery of regularities, be it in the form of chronological series or in the form of statistical relations (Boudon, 1983). Direct heirs of Durkheim's *Social Division of Labour* and *Suicide*, these theories focus on the idea that social systems should be analysed in terms of a non-random combination of characteristics (i.e. as structures). In addition, it is considered that, for Durkheim (and for most 'structuralists'), individual motivations cannot be reconstructed from a scientific point of view, and can be eliminated from social analysis without any consequences for the explanation of social phenomena.

In the same way, neo-Marxist sociologists are taken to pay very little attention to individual actors and their motivations, concentrating, instead, on showing causal and other relations of implication between various global characteristics.[1] For Boudon, this springs directly from the centrality accorded to the notion of false consciousness: if the actors' views are (mainly) false and distorted, there is not much point in integrating them in the analysis of social phenomena.

Although Boudon does not show the different assumptions inspiring neo-Durkheimians and neo-Marxists, he correctly identifies two major trends in these traditions which could justify their belonging to one single paradigm: on one level (the methodological one), sociology's method is naturalistic, in the sense that it deals with causal relations between structural elements and that this method is not different from the natural sciences'. On another level (the epistemological one), the reality of the social world is accessed through a theory of knowledge which defines (scientific) knowledge as true or, at least, as aiming at the truth. There is, however, another level which is only implicit in Boudon's characterisation of this paradigm, which is the ontological one. This is in fact what justifies the methodological level insofar as, because social structures are taken to be external and prior to individual consciousness, they are included in the natural order (Hollis, 1994).

Boudon tries to make clear that he is not completely denying the interest of such an approach. He does not deny the existence of social regularities and even suggests that the identification of causal relations between social variables may be, given the available data, the only possible approach. What he denies is that the determination of constant conjunctions is the sole, or even the most important, aim of sociology (Boudon, 1983: 305). Later on we shall see the meaning and implications of such considerations, in particular, the relations he establishes between the identification of social regularities in the form of constant conjunctions and causal relations between social variables.

The paradigm of interpretive sociology

The main characteristic of the interpretive paradigm is described in terms of the principle that sociology should not follow the traditional canons of scientific research. Contemporary thinkers who belong to this tradition tend to view the aim of social theory and social philosophy as that of identifying the relations of domination which are the basis of everyday social experience, an aim that became popular with the Frankfurt School under the name of critical theory (Boudon, 1983). The tradition is, however, much older, and its main characteristic is not so much the idea of critique (which is, in any case, not necessarily opposed to naturalism), but its anti-naturalism.

Generally speaking, interpretive social science is based on a discontinuist theory of knowledge which springs from a dualist ontology in terms of mind and Nature (Boudon, 1989b). This ontology is based on the idea that the subjects of the social sciences are significant objects which find no equivalent in the realm of Nature (Bhaskar, 1979). Boudon defends instead a continuist theory of knowledge, meaning that there is no discontinuity between the natural and the social sciences, and that the final aim of social research is also the explanation. Nonetheless, he also suggests that, depending on the nature of the available data and on the characteristics of the phenomenon in question, the explanation might seem inaccessible (normally when meaning is not directly evident) and, in this case, the analyst may offer a provisional explanation (interpretation) which may be considered as more or less appropriate. Interpretation and explanation differ in degree, not in essence: an interpretation is a weak explanation, in the sense that the former does not have the same degree of objectivity as the latter. At the same time, interpretation plays a crucial role in the social sciences because it works as a preliminary element or as a complement to explanation: '[interpretation] has a heuristic function and also a function of intelligibility' (Boudon, 1989b: 243).[2]

Interpretation is thus seen as an important element in social explanation, but its lack of objectivity makes interpretive accounts of social reality of limited applicability, and an interpretative sociology which is based on a dualist ontology should not be perceived as the aim of social research. Interpretation, as an anti-naturalistic approach, has to be differentiated from understanding. Contrary to interpretation, understanding or *Verstehen* refers not to a method that is specific to the social sciences as an alternative to that of the natural sciences, but to a particular form of explanation that relates to human action:

> The notion of understanding applies exclusively ... to the projection procedure through which the actor analyses the behaviour, the attitude, or the acts of a given individual. Thus, understanding is always the understanding of the individual actor. An individual action may be understood; a collective behaviour must be explained.
>
> (Boudon, 1989b: 243)[3]

When understanding involves not individual actions but collective phenomena, Boudon speaks of interpretation, emphasising the need for an individualistic explanation of social phenomena. The pair interpretation/explanation thus refers to the degree of objectivity present in an account of social reality, while the pair understanding/explanation refers to the level of reality to which explanation applies.

The identification Boudon establishes between objectivity and the level of analysis can be misleading. Although it is certainly true that there is a difference between the apprehension of subjectively intended meaning, on the one hand, and the historical or cultural significance of a given social phenomenon, on the other, both rely on some sort of pre-interpretation based on our natural experience of the world (in the Husserlian sense of a 'natural attitude'). Both, in a sense, represent a refusal to conform to positivist notions of objectivity, which rely on a non-mediated apprehension of reality (such as in the Vienna Circle's attempt to sharply distinguish between theoretical and observational language, and to reduce the former to the latter).

In an important sense, the interpretive tradition, especially as developed by Habermas, does not discard, or render it impossible to talk about, objectivity in the social sciences. One thing is to talk about the impossibility of objective knowledge in the logical positivist sense of the term; quite another is the impossibility of truth in terms of theoretical reason. It seems to me that Habermas contests the former, but not the latter. His critique of positivism (or, rather, of normative–analytic philosophies) is based on interpretive approaches (mainly hermeneutics) and followed by a denial of positivism's claims to universality.

According to Habermas, any theory of action has to combine assumptions that cover both the empirical context in which action happens and the logical context of symbolised meaning. In this sense, 'interpretive sociology is intended not to exclude, but to make possible adequate measurement of social facts' (Habermas, 1988: 108). Hermeneutic interpretation, in particular, is viewed as a fundamental element in the social sciences because, drawing on Gadamer's notion of understanding, it reflects a framework according to which meaning is both attributed and grasped.

The notion of framework used by both Gadamer and Habermas is holistic in principle, but, contrary to the interpretive notions of the language game and forms of life developed in Peter Winch's linguistic analysis, for instance, it does not have closed boundaries (thus rendering it impossible to compare different interpretations). Hermeneutic understanding is seen as something like a 'fusion of horizons', and this also differentiates their approach from Dilthey's hermeneutics (Hamlin, 1998). In a clear opposition to the latter's objectivistic claims, hermeneutic understanding presupposes the identification of the analyst's own framework or prejudices because they represent the basic condition of knowledge: 'our "prejudices" are not an obstacle to knowledge so much as a condition of knowledge, since they make up the fundamental structure of our relationship with our historical tradition' (Outhwaite, 1994b: 26). In this sense, prejudices should not be opposed to objectivity – in fact, Gadamer (1998) argues for the possibility of distinguishing true from false prejudices – but they constitute the very condition of objectivity:

> [The] placing of ourselves (in the situation of someone else) is not the empathy of one individual for another, nor is it the application to another person of our own criteria, but it always involves the attainment of a

higher universality that overcomes, not only our own particularity, but also that of the other. The concept of 'horizon' suggests itself because it expresses the wide, superior vision that the person who is seeking to understand must have. To acquire a horizon means that one learns to look beyond what is close at hand – not in order to look away from it, but to see it better within a larger whole and in truer proportion.

(Gadamer apud Habermas, 1988: 151–2)

As Habermas has shown, this process cannot be eliminated through methodology, i.e. it cannot be considered as a simple data selection and manipulation procedure, because it presupposes a circular relationship between pre-understanding and the explication of what is understood: 'we can decipher the parts of a text only if we anticipate an understanding, however diffuse, of the whole; and conversely, we can correct this anticipation only by explicating individual parts' (ibid.: 152). It becomes clear, then, that the importance of hermeneutic interpretation in the social sciences lies, for authors like Habermas, *in the context of meaning it provides for explanation*. But this context of meaning, is not only interpreted: it is also understood.

In this sense, Boudon's sharp differentiation between understanding and interpretation can only be attained under the following conditions:

1　That understanding can be reduced to the understanding of individual actions (genetic understanding).
2　That explanation based on that kind of understanding does not presuppose a symbolic framework according to which individuals' reasons, motives and beliefs are accounted for.

That understanding can be reduced to the understanding of individual actions is a matter of contention. Methodological individualists need to show that the understanding of the actions of individuals, their reasons, motives and beliefs, does not presuppose a (holistic) interpretation very much in accordance with Habermas's prescriptions. This possibility seems to be ruled out by Boudon himself when he characterises interpretation as a condition of intelligibility. Nonetheless, it is necessary to show that, because it is a condition of intelligibility, interpretation cannot be sharply opposed to understanding and explanation. In fact, it can be argued, hermeneutic interpretation is a condition of intelligibility which applies not only to the social, but also to the natural sciences and to human activity in general. And this is one of the criticisms which can be addressed to Habermas's anti-naturalistic perspective.

Habermas's (1988) view on the dualism of the cultural sciences suggests that the separation between understanding and interpretation as two incommensurable approaches springs from Weber's lack of clarity in distinguishing the categories of meaning (*Sinn*) and significance (*Bedeutung*).

Meaning, as subjectively intended meaning, leads to a causal explanation that is not related to hermeneutic meaning, i.e. it relates to an empirical–analytic science. But Habermas's own distinction between the social and the natural sciences suggests a fundamentally positivist conception of the natural sciences. He does in fact associate naturalism and positivism when, in his reformulation of Kant's transcendental inquiry into the possibility of knowledge, he characterises the natural sciences in term of 'technical interests in prediction and control'. According to Outhwaite (1987), Habermas's critique aimed at the intrusion of the positivist account of natural scientific methodology into the realm of social theory, which should combine the knowledge-guiding interests of the natural sciences with an interest in emancipation. This was done, however, at the expense of a critical characterisation of the natural sciences, which were conceived in positivist terms. As a result, Habermas ended up having to support:

> ... somewhat against his will, the methodological dualism, the separation of natural from social science, which had inspired the hermeneutic critique. ... [H]e did not want such a closed border between understanding and causal explanation, but he could link them only, in a rather unconvincing way, in his conception of emancipatory science based on Freudian psychoanalysis and the Marxist critique of ideology'.
>
> (ibid.: 14–5)

It is clear, however, that Boudon's contention with interpretation refers not so much to the separation it would engender between understanding and explanation, but to the impossibility of establishing its objective character on the basis of a (relatively) autonomous social order.

The neo-Weberian paradigm

Boudon (1983) identifies three main characteristics in the neo-Weberian paradigm which render it incompatible with both the neo-Durkheimian and the interpretive paradigms. First, the social sciences cannot identify general universal causes of social phenomena, but only look for singular combinations of individual reasons which are responsible for the phenomena in question. Second, because social phenomena are the result of the aggregation of individual behaviour, the actions which are at their root have to be understood according to the characteristics of the social environment of the actors. Last, but not least, understanding individual reasons and their aggregation presupposes applying the 'procedures of rational criticism' as described by philosophers in the natural sciences.

The theory of knowledge implicit in this paradigm has elements in common with both the neo-Durkheimian and the interpretive paradigms, but the way these elements are combined produces an original approach. According to Boudon, the neo-Weberian paradigm shares with the neo-Durkheimian a continuist theory of knowledge according to which there are no fundamental differences between the natural and the social sciences, and both should aim at objectivity. With the interpretive paradigm, Boudon's neo-Weberianism shares the idea that statements about reality (and he extends this notion to the natural scientific realm as well) can only be judged in terms of a general symbolic framework which contains a number of implicit arguments that often have to be questioned and analysed. This idea was presented in Chapter 2, where I described what Boudon (1990a) calls 'Simmel effects'. What I am interested in now is a particular kind of Simmel effect which refers to some epistemological a priori notions, in particular those related to the notions of truth and causality. The analysis of the first of these a priori notions will allow us to understand why Boudon believes that each of the three aforementioned paradigms has its own limited applicability and why they are normally not complementary, but incompatible. The second a priori notion will introduce the problem of causality and provide a general framework according to which explanation is dealt with in the neo-Weberian paradigm.

The uniqueness of truth

The Simmel effect deriving from the notion of truth is based on an a priori notion that is frequently used, both in the common sense and in scientific knowledge: the idea that truth is unique. According to Boudon (1990a), this principle has a *quasi*-universal quality and rests on the idea that I might have different impressions or hypotheses on what an object is, but reality can only correspond to one of these hypotheses. The importance of such a principle for both everyday and scientific knowledge goes without saying, but Boudon contests that its validity is universal: 'it often happens that many different explanations of the same phenomenon are considered as true' (ibid.: 279).[4] For this reason, he concludes, reality cannot be rendered non-existent, nor can it be reduced to being unique: it is sometimes unique, other times it is multiple.

Relying on an argument developed by Richard Rorty, Boudon argues that the principle of a unique truth can only be based on a 'mirror of Nature' conception of knowledge, that is, on a correspondence theory of knowledge which considers it as an image, in the mind, of reality such as it is. But Boudon disagrees with the sceptical solution to the problem of truth that Rorty arrives at. The true and the right are not solely matters of social practice, as neo-pragmatist approaches try to establish. In fact, he argues, all kinds of scepticism, including Rorty's, are based on the same implicit assumption that truth is unique and which takes the following form:

1) A given phenomenon **P** may engender multiple interpretations of it;
2) We cannot show that one of these interpretations is objectively preferable to the others;
3) [Truth is unique]*[5]

4) It is an illusion to talk about truth in relation to the interpretations of **P**;
5) The value of a particular interpretation of **P** cannot, in this case, rest on its truth;
6) It must, therefore, follow that it expresses other values (for instance, aesthetic values).

(Boudon, 1990a: 282–3)[6]

Boudon takes this kind of scepticism to rest entirely on two implicit propositions. The first one, proposition 5, opposes in a radical manner (through an 'abuse' of the principle of the excluded middle) objectively founded to socially founded beliefs. It also includes proposition 3, according to which truth is unique. Boudon believes that he can show with this that even those authors claiming a postmodern approach cannot easily get rid of the idea that truth is unique.

Boudon tries to show that truth is (sometimes) not unique with two examples (ibid.). The first one refers to the type of language used to describe an object: a computer, for instance, may be described either in terms of the intentions of the engineer who built it, i.e. as a machine which serves certain purposes, or in terms of its mechanisms. The argument is that the description of the computer can be accurate either in teleological or in mechanical terms, but this is not always the case, for some types of explanation do not make sense in a teleological language.

In the second example, Boudon refers to the neo-Kantian thesis of the infinite complexity of reality and the need to select particular aspects of it if any knowledge is to be possible. One of the implications of this thesis is that it is impossible to identify all the causal chains involved in the determination of a certain state of affairs. In this sense, all explanations would involve a choice of certain causal chains considered relevant for the phenomenon in question, that is, it involves an interpretative moment. This possibility of choice is what renders the existence of multiple truths possible. But what lies behind the possibility of choice is the more basic idea that it is impossible to grasp the true essence of any object, since its description also involves a selection of certain of its aspects. This means that the notion of truth is related to the description of certain elements under a particular perspective. Since there are almost as many perspectives as there are knowing subjects, he concludes, there may be many different truths.

Objective knowledge, according to this perspective, would be a kind of socially founded belief whose objectivity is relative to both a specific context and to the theory adopted. This is Boudon's position when he distinguishes between good reasons and objective rationality. Good reasons should be analysed in terms of 'market products': 'The reasons to believe that "any movement is the effect of a physical force" are good in the sense that, no objections being raised against this principle …, there is no effectively available argument in the market capable of weakening it' (Boudon, 1996d: 380).

But in order that such argument is not mistaken for the pragmatist conclusion which Boudon criticises in Rorty's approach, it is important to differentiate it from the 'epistemic fallacy', i.e. the idea that being can be analysed in terms of our knowledge of it or, that since our knowledge is contingent, that which it expresses must also be contingent. This would be to conflate the epistemological and the ontological domains, or to say that the way things are depends both on what human beings are (their cognitive abilities) and on how they represent things. According to the epistemic fallacy, the natural and the social orders are conceived in terms of human constructs imposed by the cognitive activities of human beings, and not as something which can have an independent reality (Bhaskar, 1997).

The differentiation between epistemic and ontological relativism lies in the possibility of the transcendental establishment of reality, or on the establishment of what the world must be like for knowledge of it to be possible at all. This means that it is possible to know that something exists even though we may not be able to describe it. This is what Bhaskar (1991: 27) tries to do when he argues that, from a transcendental realist perspective, 'reality can be unequivocally (and no longer anthropocentrically or epistemologically) accorded to things. ... the way things are in the world takes no particular account of how humans are, or whether and how they choose to represent them'.

This should not lead to the conclusion that a notion like 'truth' is not particularly ambiguous. Its ambiguity derives, among other things, from the possibility of describing objects, as well as explaining phenomena, in different ways. As with Boudon's argument above, it is possible to use different languages to describe an object, but some descriptions are accurate and others are not. The particular problem this brings about is that sometimes it is not possible to decide between alternative descriptions, but the ambiguity of our knowledge should not be mistaken for the ambiguity of reality. In fact, it is only because things exist in reality independently of the way we describe them that we can speak of the fallibility of knowledge: 'To be a fallibilist about knowledge, it is necessary to be a realist about things. Conversely, to be a sceptic about things is to be a dogmatist about knowledge' (Bhaskar, 1997: 43). In other words, there is no incompatibility between ontological realism (provided we do not mistake philosophical for scientific realism) and an epistemological relativism of the type described above.

The socially founded character of knowledge does not entail the socially founded character of reality, in the sense of this reality being dependent on the language used in its description. Only the conflation of these two levels would allow for the possibility of concluding, from the (true) idea that reality cannot be evaluated independently of the language employed in its definition, the (false) idea that different descriptions of an object entail the existence of different realities, hence, of different truths.

This can be illustrated with Boudon's own differentiation between genetic and functional paradigms. Functional and genetic *explanation* are considered as alternatives to each other and, although Boudon believes that some types of social phenomena can be explained in both languages, only the use of the a priori notion of unique truth would make it possible to view them as complementary to each other.

The main distinction between genetic and functional paradigms is made in terms of synchronic and diachronic analysis. Functional paradigms explain social phenomena without any (causal) reference to historical data, which, incidentally, brings about the characterisation of neo-Weberianism as a type of functional analysis. An important example of functional analysis is Weber's explanation of the strength of Protestant sects in the United States. For Weber, the United States differs from many European nations in a number of traits, such as less marked symbols of social stratification, and a more equalitarian ideology. On the religious level, whereas nations like Germany or France had a dominant Church, the United States was characterised by a number of sects. Also, the elite in that country were mainly Protestant. All these elements are combined to explain the structure of American religious life in terms of a language that deals exclusively with the elements in the system of stratification which were present at the moment of the analysis.

The same phenomenon may also be appropriately explained through a genetic language. In that case, the analyst would probably look for the interconnection of past conjunctural and structural elements and events which led to the present state of affairs. For Boudon (1990a), the same *explanandum* may generate 'different truths' which are complementary and juxtaposed to each other, but the history of the social sciences shows instead that the two languages normally produce deeply antithetic results, and normally only one of these results can lead to true theories.

From this, he concludes that there is no general answer to the question of the appropriate language for social and historical phenomena: some questions engender objective and unique answers, while others do not. And because there is no way of knowing a priori whether the *explanandum* in question admits to more than one answer, the appropriate language for the explanation of a phenomenon cannot be judged on the ontological level, but only on the methodological one.

Contrary to that, I believe that the independence between description and explanation is only relative because, as Harré and Madden (1998) have shown, there is an intrinsic relation between what an object is, and what it is capable of doing and suffering. In other words, the difference in language does not necessarily entail different truths, but different languages entail different *explananda* which, in their turn, may entail different *explanans*. But either the definition of the *explanandum* and the characterisation of the *explanans* is true, or it is not: the important point in terms of differences in language is that some descriptions of the *explananda* may be appropriate or not, right or wrong. These descriptions, in their turn, have to relate to some ontology to the extent that the ontological level refers to the predicates which are considered appropriate to the description and explanation of objects. Now, the argument that it is not possible to establish the truth of alternative theories is not under dispute here: what is being emphasised is that the ambivalence of our knowledge should not be equated to the ambivalence of the real world.

Everything has a cause

The role interpretation plays in neo-Weberian analysis can only be fully understood along with the type of (functional) explanation which characterises it. Because any account of explanation involves a definition of causality, I will introduce this subject with a brief analysis of another type of Simmel effect: the idea that everything has a cause. The importance of this type of effect refers both to the possibility of inferring from there a definition of causality, and to the possibility of establishing the ontological consequences which spring from such definition.

According to Boudon (1990a), the idea that everything has a cause is an epistemological a priori notion (in the sense of a conjecture) which deserves investigation. He starts this investigation by analysing the Kantian principle according to which the statement 'everything has a cause' is a *synthetic* a priori *judgement*. According to his reading of Kant, it is a priori because it is not dictated by experience, but it allows us to organise our experiences of the world. It is synthetic because, contrary to analytic judgements, it does not refer to the meaning of the concepts which are being used to describe reality, but to reality itself. Boudon contests the Kantian classification of that conjecture in terms of a synthetic a priori notion: 'Every event has a cause' is not an analytic principle, because it is not possible to deduce it directly from the notion of event, and it is not an *a posteriori* proposition, because it is not derived from experience. As it is neither analytic nor a posteriori, it does not follow that it is a synthetic a priori notion. For a proposition to belong to the class of synthetic judgements it has to inform us that reality is constituted in a certain way which excludes some others, and it is impossible to imagine a state of things that would contradict the judgement 'every event has a cause'(ibid.: 237).

Consider, for instance, a case in which I have established that A is the cause of B because I repeatedly observed that relation in reality. If I face a situation in which A is not the cause of B, it cannot be concluded that every event does not have a cause, but perhaps that there were hidden causes in the case in question which I could not identify. Even in the situation where I cannot find any causes for a phenomenon, it does not necessarily follow that not every event has a cause. With these examples Boudon concludes that the famous proposition 'every event has a cause' is neither analytic nor synthetic, rather it has the status of a conjecture that helps us organise our experiences about the world.[7] For this reason, the notion of cause is rendered irreparably obscure and ambiguous.

Boudon's argument seems to rest entirely on a conflation between the domain of the real (which comprises experiences, events and mechanisms) and the domain of the actual (which comprises experiences and events). In fact, the equivalence he establishes between the propositions 'everything has a cause' and 'every event has a cause' points to that conflation and suggests the adoption of a perspective which Bhaskar terms 'actualism'. According to Bhaskar (1997: 64), the term 'actualism' refers to the doctrine of the actuality of causal laws or 'to the idea that laws are relations between events or states of affairs (which are thought to constitute the objects of actual or possible experiences)'. In this sense, according to actualism, we cannot know the *modus operandi* of things, only their relations (of similitude or succession) to other things.

For Boudon it is impossible to give an objective definition of the notion of cause because its definition rests on 'cognitive interests': depending on the interests involved in the research, someone can select, among a variety of causes, one that will count as *the* cause of the phenomenon he/she wants to explain. Accordingly, in some cases the cause attributed to a phenomenon can be considered as the *accident* which disturbed a 'normal' course of events. Alternatively, the attributed cause may refer to an underlying state (disposition) of the social actors involved in the event. What seems to be at stake in the notion of interest is a pragmatist conception of knowledge according to which the context-relativity of explanation rules out its definition in terms of the establishment of an objective (in the sense of being independent of the human subject) relation between events. But it should be considered that, although the (cognitive) interests which guide explanation do affect the notion of objectivity in scientific knowledge, they do not affect it to such an extent that the transcendence of particular contexts becomes impossible (Bhargava, 1992). There are validating norms in scientific inquiry (such as rational justification) which adapt themselves to different types of *explananda* (and of cognitive interests).

Boudon's conception of cognitive interests is intimately related to the idea that it is difficult to establish a precise boundary to the causal relations which engender a certain state of affairs. In principle, it is always possible to regress *ad infinitum* to more basic causes, but this possibility cannot be considered for practical purposes. In this sense, a causal imputation always involves a choice which rests on more or less well-founded principles which may, in their turn, be only implicit. The choices available can be in great number, and they are often dictated not by reality, but by epistemological, logical and ontological a priori notions (Boudon, 1990a).

Following Popper, Boudon (1990a) does not believe that the existence of these frameworks makes objective knowledge impossible: faulty or poor a priori notions often lead to some sort of dead end and make it impossible to deal with the questions the researcher has in mind. But Boudon disagrees with Popper's view that this is always the case. In many cases reality does not exclude a particular frame, and the knowing subject may use some commonsense notions which, despite being very simple and providing apparently powerful explanations, are flawed. Two cases illustrate this situation. The first one concerns the problem of why we often underestimate the complexity of networks of causality and attribute the cause of a phenomenon to one single element. The second case tries to explain why we often attribute causes to contingent phenomena, i.e. to phenomena which are accidental and which have no cause. Reducing multiple causal relations to a single one often involves a reasoning that takes the form:

1) [Q has *a* cause]*
2) What is the cause of Q?
3) [A *real* cause possesses the property S]*
4) P has the property S
5) P is *a real* cause of Q

___

6) P is *the* cause of Q.

(Boudon, 1990a: 248)[8]

The propositions contained in [ ]* are a priori notions. Proposition 1 legitimates question 2 in the eyes of the knowing subject. Proposition 3 is a particular account of the notion of cause. The conjunction of 1 and 3 may give a particular cause the status of an unique cause, and 3 might take various forms, such as S = the ability to set in motion an inert system; S = the ability to put a system into an abnormal state; S = the property of always being present whenever the effect Q appears; S = a necessary condition for the appearance of Q; S = a sufficient condition for the appearance of Q; S = the representation of the essence (in the philosophical sense) of the system in which Q appears; or S = a contingent element which we may try to eliminate.

The particular forms which the notion of cause assumes may relate not only to the logical relations attributed to them, but also to what Boudon calls ontological definitions of cause, i.e. they may incorporate the idea that the true causes of a phenomenon are always situated in a particular sector of reality: for some, ideas are what rule the world, for others, interests, relations of production, etc. Whatever the form of the a priori notion in question, they share the characteristic of 'going beyond' reality. And they show that an epistemological principle such as that of unique causes can only be rendered possible by the adoption of a particular and restrictive definition of cause. Moreover, they show that what allows for the substitution of the indefinite article 'a' (a cause) for the definite article 'the' (the cause) is a choice which rules out other possibilities and which is based on implicit (logical, ontological, linguistic) principles which are taken for granted, sometimes generating false inferences.

The second case refers to why we tend to attribute causal relations where they do not exist. Here Boudon argues that the notion that 'everything has a cause' precludes us from considering contingent phenomena when they happen. A contingent phenomenon, for him, is the result of the encounter of two (or more) independent causal chains and, in this sense, it refers to what we normally call an accident. Although some events can be clearly and easily attributed to a Cournot effect, i.e. they can be viewed as the accidental product of the encounter of independent causal series, others are not easily so. This is particularly true of cases in which strong statistical correlations between phenomena are observed.

The example Boudon (1990a) uses to illustrate this case is a study by S. Steinberg, *The American Melting Pot*, where the author shows some strong statistical relations between the speciality of university professors and their religious affiliation. The research shows a strong representation of Protestants in the classical scientific disciplines, such as agronomy, chemistry, botany and zoology. Protestants are under-represented in the social sciences and the humanities. Catholics, in their turn, are strongly represented in the humanities, and Jews in the social sciences, from anthropology to psychology, economics, political science and social work. Disciplines such as medicine, physics, biochemistry and bacteriology have a low proportion of Jews.

The distribution of these data hardly suggest a random process. On the contrary, they suggest some sort of 'affinity' between religious affiliation and the disciplines chosen by each group, even though certain categories do not fit so easily into the pattern just described: the Protestant group is shown to dominate musical disciplines; the Catholics, the fine-arts; and the Jews have a tendency to choose certain natural sciences, but not others. These data are, however, interpreted in terms of the 'plausible assumption' that every statistical correlation holds deviant cases; therefore the former correlations are not really questioned.

Steinberg interprets these data with the aid of a cultural theory according to which the ethos of each religious group guides individual professional choices: the humanities are more in accordance with the axiological orientation of Catholics; the natural sciences and technical professions have an ascetic dimension which is in accordance with the values to which Protestants subscribe; Jews tend to choose those disciplines with a strong component of 'human relations' because of the values they were taught in their childhood and adolescence.

Boudon attributes the wide acceptance of such a culturalist interpretation to three main factors. In the first place, the observed correlations are strong, giving the impression that they are easily and readily understood, since one can almost immediately detect the similarities between the disciplines which characterise each religious group. Second, this type of correlation was the object of a number of well-established studies, following a tradition initiated by Max Weber in *The Protestant Ethic* and continued by authors such as Merton. Third, an alternative to such an interpretation does not present itself so easily, especially if this alternative involves attributing a Cournot effect to the observed statistical correlation. In other words, Boudon tries to establish that strong statistical relations do not necessarily represent causal relations, and his argument is developed as follows.

Following the increase in the social mobility of the American Jewish community, when a youngster of this group was confronted with a university education and career, the social sciences, the humanities, law and medicine, were expanding courses. Although he considers the fact that the social mobility of the North American Jewish community and the expansion of those courses coincided in time is not necessarily the result of a random process, Boudon interprets the encounter of the two causal series as an accident: the increase in the demand by the Jewish community for university courses and the increase in the offer of certain courses is a contingent phenomenon, and the Jewish under-representation in the humanities is the product of chance.

The Protestants' choices are explained in the same fashion: whereas at their origin the university teaching staff are almost always Protestant, the disciplines which have more places available are those which correspond to the more immediate social, economic and religious needs. In this sense, the older well-established disciplines (zoology, botany, music) display a strong representation of Protestants, whereas the newer ones, such as biochemistry or bacteriology, have a high proportion of Jews. The idea is then to explain the Cournot effect in this case in terms of the variation of the structure of the opportunities in time, on the one hand, and the demand of certain groups, on the other.

Apart from this interpretation, the cultural theory proposed can be undermined on a different ground. It is easy to observe that the correlations between disciplines and religious affiliation are not stable over time. And this lack of stability is, according to Boudon, not compatible with the notion of fixed cultural choices based on an ethos. Moreover, it is easier to reconstruct the representation of groups once we relate it not to the content of the different disciplines, but to the history of their expansion. This would allow us, for instance, to notice that the social mobility of the Jews contributed to the expansion of disciplines related to the social sciences. It would also make it possible to conclude that both Catholics and Jews are absent from those disciplines characterised by a low rate of belief, and present in those characterised by a high rate of belief, provided the two groups are characterised by significant social mobility (Boudon, 1990a: 270).

It seems to me that what this example shows is not so much that there is not a causal relation between religious affiliation and professional choice, but rather that this causal relation is mediated by other (contingent) factors which need to be taken into account if the relation is to make any sense. In this sense, the causal relation is not absent or spurious, but certain conditions (i.e. social mobility of the groups in question) have to occur for the relation to manifest itself at the actual level. This characterises what Boudon calls functional explanation, considered by him as a quasi-causal explanation, given the contingent actualisation of the relation.

Functional and historical approaches in the neo-Weberian explanation of action

The characterisation of the neo-Weberian paradigm as representing a type of functional analysis is a puzzling idea, but only insofar as no distinction is made between functional analysis and functionalism. In Chapter 2, I tried to show Boudon's distinction between functional systems (based on the notion of role), and systems of interdependence. According to Boudon (1979: 111), the conflation between functional analysis and functionalism can only be made if all systems of interaction are taken to be role systems. Moreover, some types of functionalism (hyperfunctionalism) add to this conflation the implicit idea that functional systems do not allow for any autonomy of the actors in terms of their interpretations of, and of conformity to, roles. His idea of functional analysis agrees with none of these propositions, thus guaranteeing a certain degree of individual autonomy in relation to social systems. It is this autonomy that makes it necessary for the choices that are made by individuals to be understood and explained.

This definition of functional analysis renders Boudon's individualism essentially explanatory (although this does not invalidate the fact that it is also ontological, or that it has some important ontological consequences), but its explanatory character has to be distinguished from another kind of explanatory individualism, that represented by Jon Elster. According to Boudon (1990a: 290), the form which functional analysis assumes in his individualism has a non-metaphorical sense, a sense which is considered by Elster to be possible, but not common in social theory (Elster, 1983; 1993).

For Elster (1993: 28), functional explanation in the social sciences 'rests upon an ill-conceived analogy from biology', and a closer analysis of that kind of explanation shows that the analogy does not hold. Functional explanation in biology is based on the theory of natural selection and states that, while mutations are random, the selection process of these mutations by a species is deterministic: 'the mutation is accepted if the first organism in which it occurs benefits in the form of higher reproductive capacity' (Elster, 1983: 50). This deterministic process makes it possible to argue that a natural selection process in the form of a genetic mutation, an environmental change, etc., is functional to an organism if it increases the reproductive capacity of this organism. Moreover, functionalism, in biology, makes it possible to understand why particular organisms present particular features if it can be shown 'that a small change in the feature in question will lead to reduced reproductive capacity for the organism' (ibid.: 53).

The inadequacy of such a model for the social sciences is shown through a comparison between the behavioural characteristics of biological organisms, on the one hand, and of social individuals, on the other. Elster characterises biological organisms as 'locally maximizing machines', meaning that if ever the organisms in a population reject all the possible mutations presented to them, these organisms have reached a local *maximum*. They cannot wait and say 'no' to a favourable mutation, for instance, in order to say 'yes' to an even more favourable one in the future. Human beings, on the other hand, are capable of waiting and using indirect strategies (such as learning from past unsuccessful experiences, pre-committing themselves in order to reduce the set of feasible choices in the future, etc.) and, in this sense, they can be characterised as 'globally maximising machines' (Elster, 1993).

According to Elster (1983:55), the attraction that many social scientists have for functional explanation stems from the implicit assumption that all social and psychological phenomena must have a meaning, i.e. that there must be some sense, some perspective in which they are beneficial for someone or something, and that furthermore these beneficial effects are what explain the phenomena in question.

However, Elster distinguishes between a weak and a strong functionalist programme in social theory, and the former is not necessarily incompatible with the explanation of social phenomena. The strong programme rests on a principle advanced by Malinowski which is described in the following terms: 'all social phenomena have beneficial consequences (intended or unintended, recognized or unrecognized) that explain them' (ibid.: 57). The weak programme involves Merton's idea that 'whenever social phenomena have consequences that are beneficial, unintended and unrecognized, they can also be explained by these consequences' (ibid.). According to Elster, Merton's principle deviates from what is considered to be a valid form of functional explanation, which, were it to be valid, should take the following form:

An institution or a behavioural pattern X is explained by its function Y for group Z if and only if:

1) Y is an effect of X;
2) Y is beneficial for Z;
3) Y is unintended by the actors producing X;
4) Y (or at least the causal relationship between X and Y) is un-recognized by the actors in Z;
5) Y maintains X by a causal feedback loop passing though Z.

(Elster, 1983: 57)

The main problem Elster sees with the application of this model to the social sciences is that, whenever criteria 1–4 are fulfilled, criterion 5 is tacitly presupposed. The problem with this presupposition is that, in the social sciences, the feedback loop normally assumes the form of an objective teleology, 'a process that has no subject, yet has a goal', or the idea that a given institution or behavioural pattern is the means to an certain end (ibid.: 59). Teleological explanation can only make sense in the context of subjective intentionality and, for this reason, a functionalist explanation cannot really explain what its proponents are aiming at.

Despite this strong opposition to a functional explanation, Elster leaves open the question whether Merton's analyses can be included in the aforementioned pattern. For him, it is not clear whether Merton's functional analyses are intended to explain social phenomena, or merely represent a paradigm for the establishment of unintended consequences of social action.

Boudon's answer to that seems to refer to the latter possibility (at least in relation to what he considers as important in Merton's functionalism). According to him, the notion of function has suffered a radical reformulation in the social sciences which has led to its dissolution as such: 'the notion of function ... is undergoing decomposition because of the very progress of research. Coming as it does from a spontaneous epistemology it cannot be incorporated within a scientific language without fundamental reformulation' (Boudon, 1980: 199). From the absolute functionalism of Malinowski and Radcliffe-Brown, to the relativised functionalism of Parsons and Merton, functional analysis has lost its meaning as an analogue of the biological concept. Whereas absolute functionalism takes for granted a notion of function which cannot be unequivocally defined, modern structural–functionalism does away altogether with the notion of function as its basic concept of explanation, and rests instead on an argument that assumes the following form:

1) A feature A implies circumstances a, b...n.
2) A feature B implies circumstances a', b' ... m.
3) Circumstances a and a', for example, are incompatible.
4) Hence: features A and B cannot be present simultaneously within a society.

(ibid.: 201)

Functional analysis rests on showing either the impossibility of the co-occurrence of two (or more) antagonistic elements, or the necessity of the co-occurrence of certain elements in a social system. But showing the necessity or the impossibility of the co-occurrence of certain elements is indeed *explaining* their relations. Boudon seems to make a distinction between these things by arguing that, although it is possible to demonstrate without many problems the impossibility of that co-occurrence, it is more difficult to accept demonstrations of necessity. Insofar as Parsons and Merton seem to have had a diffuse consciousness of this difficulty in their functional analyses, they have rarely tried to establish causal relations of the type 'if A, then B'. For Boudon, thus, the difference between the two kinds of functional analyses lies in the fact that, whereas modern structural analysis (normally) leads to negative demonstrations (the impossibility of the co-occurrence of certain elements within a social system), classical or absolute functionalism leads to pseudo-demonstrations of necessity. From this he concludes that structural–functional analyses, when they are valid, are not explanatory. Their importance refers instead to the understanding of the objective constraints and enabling conditions which individuals face:

Some of these structures amplify the agents' aims, some send them back *(les retournent)*, some respect their aims but produce different, undesired, effects. Certain structures produce collective states of tension which do not result from the antagonism of interests. Others, indirectly produce collective positive effects which the agents would not be capable of actualising had they tried to directly obtain them. Still, others are responsible for global social changes which take the form of true collective innovations.

(Boudon, 1979: 158)[9]

Functional analysis is thus viewed by Boudon in terms of the contribution it brings to the interpretation of the objective conditions of action and according to which meaning is attributed. They are, in this sense, the *causes* of the mental processes which lead to action. But these causes cannot be identified with the direct causes of social phenomena, as if there was a historical subject which acts teleologically. In this restricted sense, functional analysis is the 'functional' equivalent of historical approaches which try to determine the contexts in which certain rules and beliefs make sense to individual actors. It provides a context of meaning which helps to understand/ explain individual actions.

This brings me to the problem of history in the explanation of action. Boudon takes the relation between history and sociology to be a complex one, and it is sometimes impossible to decide whether a particular study belongs to the realm of one or the other discipline (Boudon and Bourricaud, 1982). Their intricate relations forbid a differentiation in terms of nomothetic and idiographic disciplines: sociology can be either, depending on the aims of the researcher. The histories of these disciplines show, nonetheless, some specificities according to which one can distinguish a number of characteristic traits in terms of aims and methods belonging to history and sociology.

The first of these traits relates to the fact that the sociologist, more often than the historian, searches for the causes of a macro-social phenomenon by isolating it from its historical flux. The second trait is the sociologists' aspiration to generality. This last characteristic requires clarification, so as not to be identified with the general distinction between nomothetic and idiographic disciplines.

The generality characterising sociology can be understood in terms of three different programmes. The first one refers to the search for (functional) 'general laws' which take the form '$y = f(x)$', or '$y = f(x_1, x_2,$ etc.$)$' (Boudon and Bourricaud, 1982: 281). Boudon takes this kind of 'law' to have an extremely local character, and its validity conditions are difficult to specify. In this sense, they are not really general laws, but conditional ones. This limitation in the programme relativises the distinction between sociology and history in terms of the nomothetic character of the latter.

The second programme manifests itself in the form of the search for 'evolutive laws'. These 'laws' do not establish a causal relation between two (or more) variables, but they postulate that a system has to go through a number of stages which are determined in advance. Just like conditional laws, evolutive laws have a local, rather than a general, character. They are true in certain contexts and under certain conditions which are also difficult to specify. In an important sense, evolutionism coincides with historicism, and it is often difficult to establish precise boundaries between sociology and history based on this model, unless the idea of law is removed from the historical realm (which is not necessarily the case in historicism).

The third programme, the most fertile in Boudon's view, represents the study of structural models. Instead of looking for conditional general laws or evolutive laws, the structural model programme provides the analytical tools for the construction of models which, provided there is an appropriate characterisation of each case, may apply to social phenomena which, from a purely phenomenal perspective, are very distinct from each other. The analysis of singular phenomena (whether they take the form of a historical event, of the existence of particular social group, or of a characteristic peculiar to one society) is interpreted in terms of the singular manifestation of more general structures. But instead of dissolving history into sociology, the differentiation between the two disciplines will probably rest on the degree of generalisation involved in each analysis. The distinction is blurred and relative to the time span considered in each case, and its precise boundaries are not always definable.

Generally speaking, the structural model programme represents a genetic approach which, based on Popper, Boudon calls 'historism'. Historism is, in a sense, the opposite of historicism: instead of looking for laws of historical development, it refers to the 'trivial' idea that culture and all human institutions are in perpetual change. In its extreme form, this idea is taken to mean that history aims at the study of concrete and singular individualities, excluding the study of any structural regularities. According to this perspective, not only would history be purely descriptive or idiographic, but the basis for this descriptive character would make impossible any type of generalisation. Boudon does not accept this extreme form and relies, instead, on the concept of a model.

According to him, a model has a double property: it is general, in the sense that it can be applied to a variety of space–time contexts, and it is ideal, in the sense that it does not strictly apply to any concrete situation. It should, therefore, be distinguished from a law which, according to him, represents an empirical statement (thus contrasting with the ideal character of the model) and is universal (contrasting with its generality). In this differentiation, Boudon approvingly quotes Simmel in arguing that 'the obsession of absolutely trying to find "laws" of social life … is nothing but a retreat into the philosophical belief of ancient metaphysicians, according to which knowledge has to be absolutely universal and necessary' (Simmel *apud* Boudon and Bourricaud, 1982: 523–4).[10]

Contrary to historism, historicism can be characterised as the search for laws of history. It may assume different forms, depending, for instance, on whether these laws are taken to be the result of a natural development of human nature, or the natural development of tendencies inscribed in the structural properties of particular social organisations. Whatever its form, historicism is characterised by a postulate of a natural and necessary succession of stages which are often verified in a tautological way. In this sense, Boudon argues, social systems are considered as closed and operating under constant conditions (Boudon and Bourricaud, 1982: 287).

Once again, because the neo-Kantian approach which informs historism is not confined to history, the differentiation between history and sociology in terms of generalisations is also relativised. It is also important to note that Boudon does not deny the heuristic character of those different programmes insofar as both history and sociology have sometimes to aim at different types of analysis. Those different programmes can, in this sense, render historical and sociological phenomena more intelligible, provided all of them are conceived in terms of *descriptive laws* and differentiated from *causal statements*. In all the cases above, when methodological individualism is applicable, the real causes are going to be established at the level of agency, with the aid of that descriptive context. When it is not, the analysis stops at the macro-level, and the 'explanations' they provide are not real explanations because they are not based on the establishment of 'real causes'.

The ambiguous nature attributed to the notion of cause, together with the role of structural models in explanation, make it possible to conclude that one of Boudon's main contentions with the causal relation which can be established between structure and agency (which is supposed to ground the notion of a socially and practically determined subject) refers to problems intrinsic to a Humean notion of causality.

Given his anti-realism, Boudon does not distinguish causal from other types of correlation on the basis of natural necessity; given his denial that cause is a primitive idea which is directly intelligible (an a priori notion), that distinction cannot be made in terms of logical necessity either. In this sense, all that remains is the Humean idea that causal regularities or laws 'can be explicated without recourse to irreducible modal notions' (Halfpenny, 1982: 70). This idea is particularly problematic because it does not allow for the distinction between causal and accidental relations, and insofar as the Humean notions of necessary and sufficient conditions cannot account for causal relations, Boudon's denial of the existence of sociological and historical laws based on their contingent (as opposed to necessary) character does not hold.[11]

Apart from the impossibility of differentiating causal or lawful regularities from accidental ones based on the necessary (logical or material) relations between a cause and its effects, Boudon also faces the problem of having to determine the 'real' character of the causes which can be established at the level of agency. The solution he gives to this problem lies in the adoption of a modified Humean account of causal relations, developed by Donald

Davidson, and according to which no (direct) reference to a law is necessary for the establishment of a causal relation. The Davidsonian conception of causality constitutes the basis of another type of explanatory individualism: that developed by Jon Elster. In this sense, a comparison between Elster's and Boudon's approach to individual explanation may be enlightening.

The Davidson–Elster account of social explanation: reasons as causes

Jon Elster's methodological individualism can be defined as an explanatory approach which rests on the philosophical system developed by Donald Davidson. According to Bhargava (1992: 127) the justification for individualism as an explanatory device rests on the idea that 'all action is analytically intentional and intentions are mental and uniquely individual entities'. For Elster (1983), this view entails a type of explanation which differs both from the causal model used in (pre-relativistic and pre-quantum-theoretical) physics, and from the functionalist causal model used in biology: intentional behaviour can also be causally explained, but only in individualistic terms.

In broad terms, the model comes from Davidson's idea that intentional action cannot be taken to rise above the causal level: 'the ordinary notion of cause is essential to the understanding of what it is to act with a reason, to have a certain intention in acting, to act counter to one's own best judgement, or to act freely' (Davidson, 1980: XI). However, mental events cannot be subsumed to general physical (deterministic) laws because psychological states involve the assumption of cognitive structures which are as complex as language structures, and the former cannot be understood without the latter. In this sense, Davidson's position in relation to the mind–body problem is described by Elster (1983: 22) as materialist, but not reductionist: mental states are only brain states, but they cannot be extensionally reduced to brain states.[12]

Because Davidson subscribes to the Humean notion of causality (in the sense that causal statements entail laws), there is a paradox in defining human actions as part of the natural realm, on the one hand, and denying that mental events can be explained in terms of deterministic laws, on the other. According to John Passmore (1985: 65), Davidson's solution to this paradox lies in an ontology of events based on the idea that 'the same act can be intentional under some description, and unintentional under a different description – as I might intentionally write a Polish name but unintentionally spell it wrong, without performing two distinct acts'. The logical form of a sentence describing such an act does not explicitly determine 'what sentences it entails and what sentences it is entailed by' (Davidson, 1980: 140), because different definitions of the *explanandum* entail different forms of explanation. This lack of clarity makes Davidson argue for a description of sentences (relating to both actions and events) in such a way as to represent the particular, unrepeatable and dated character of events.

The basis of this ontology of events lies in the (Humean) idea that 'causes and effects are entities that can be named or described in singular terms; probably events, since one can follow another' (ibid.: 149). Moreover, whenever different objects produce the same effect, this must be due to the existence of some common quality: 'like effects imply like causes, [and] we must always ascribe the causation to the circumstances, wherein we discover the resemblance' (Hume *apud* Davidson, 1980: 149). Nonetheless, because there is the possibility of describing the same phenomenon in different languages, Davidson concludes that there must be a distinction between causes and the features used for describing them. This distinction allows for a further differentiation between statements which establish in a non-equivocal way that some event caused another, and statements which allow for the deduction that the relation between two or more events was causal.

Such deduction normally follows from general laws, but Davidson believes that causal laws are not indispensable for singular causal and intentional statements. Hume's notion of causality as entailing laws can be interpreted in two different ways: 'it may mean that "A caused B" entails some particular law involving the predicates used in the descriptions "A" and "B", or it may mean that "A caused B" entails that there exists a causal law instantiated by some true descriptions of A and B' (ibid.: 16). The second interpretation gives a much weaker account of the idea that causal statements entail laws because 'no particular law is entailed by a singular causal claim, and a singular causal claim can be defended, if it needs defence, without defending any law' (ibid., 17). Since the law which connects two events is not necessarily connecting them under the descriptions we use to assert the causal connection, Davidson's thesis is that act-statements do instantiate causal laws *when correctly reduced to events*, but not when they appear in intentional statements (Passmore, 1988).

According to Elster, an important consequence of Davidson's views on mental states is that actions are caused by beliefs and desires, but we have to bear in mind that stating that a belief or a desire is the cause of an action is only a convenient way of rephrasing the intentional explanation 'in such a way as to indicate the existence of some (unknown) causal explanation'. For practical purposes, the distinction between causal and intentional explanation should be maintained because, although the former allows for us to 'talk about all there is, including mental phenomena', it does not allow us to 'single out mental phenomena from what else there is' (Elster, 1983: 22).

The importance of isolating mental phenomena is because it provides an element for showing how individual judgement and autonomy are possible, on the one hand, and what is the nature of the relation (logical and/or causal) between this autonomy and individual behaviour. The logical relation between intentions and behaviour shows that there is a possibility that the behaviour in question is an action, by establishing that the individual acted with the intention of bringing about a certain state of affairs. The causal relation shows that the action did indeed occur, and that it did not remain a mere possibility (Bhargava, 1992). The logical relation between intentions and behaviour also provides an important paradigm for the explanation of irrational behaviour, since it can be shown that, although there were intentions involved in the behaviour, those intentions did not bring about the desired or expected consequences. This can be shown not through a causal analysis, but through an analysis of inconsistent beliefs and desires.[13]

For Elster, there are two levels in which causality is involved in the explanation of social phenomena, apart from intentional explanation. First, there is the level of the formation of beliefs and desires which is termed by him 'sub-intentional causality'.[14] Second, there is a 'supra-intentional' causal level represented by the interaction between intentional actors, which is exemplified in most accounts of unintended consequences of action.

The focus on sub-intentional causality is probably the most striking difference between Elster and Boudon. The latter's theory of cognitive rationality rests on the possibility of explaining the adherence to beliefs in the same way that action is explained. For Elster, who also concentrates on the role of desires for the determination of action, socialisation processes are an important element of social analysis. Although, like Boudon, Elster does not take socialisation to be the direct precursor of action, it plays an important role in the understanding of the conditions of the actors: 'first a causal explanation of desires, then an intentional explanation of action in terms of the desires, and finally a causal explanation of macro-states in terms of the several individual actions' (ibid.: 85).

Understanding action thus involves, for Elster, causal and intentional explanation. Understanding why the actors behave as they do involves showing 'for the sake of what goal' they behave in a certain way (Elster, 1983: 84). Here, Elster seems to have two different approaches: the first one relates to Davidson's position that identifying beliefs and desires involves the *simultaneous* interpretation of actors' speech and explanation of their actions:

> ... it is not reasonable to suppose we can interpret verbal behaviour without fine-grained information about beliefs and intentions, nor is it reasonable to imagine we can justify the attribution of preferences among complex options unless we can interpret speech behaviour. A radical theory of decision must include a theory of interpretation and cannot presuppose it.
>
> (Davidson, 1984: 147)

The second one relates to Elster's idea that the explanation of beliefs and desires can be accessed though the hermeneutic method, which is taken by him to be a sub-species of the hypothetico-deductive method or 'the hypothetico-deductive method applied to intentional phenomena, with some peculiar features due to the nature of these phenomena' (Elster, 1983: 16–17).

Either way, the causal mechanisms involved in the determination of desires and beliefs entail that action cannot be fully accounted in individualistic terms; although meaning cannot exist without individual consciousness, nor can consciousness exist without individual realisation, meaning is not restricted to that (Bhargava, 1992). In fact, the very idea of practical inference presupposes an interpretation of meaning according to the practical rules of a given community. This poses a serious threat to all individualistic approaches because, whereas these approaches rest on the assumption that beliefs, values, desires, and the like, are mental entities and, as such, can only be grasped in terms of individual mental contents, meaning can only be attributed as part of a particular language game which is social in character. As Bhaskar (1979: 147) has put the matter, 'intentions are personal, meanings are social'. In Bhargava's (1992: 200) words:

> ... belief-contents are dependent upon the usages of words in a society and cannot be individuated in a context-independent way. Hence, they are social. If this is correct, it follows that belief-content is not just a matter of an internal psychological state the attribution of which is independent of the character of the social world. While the ascription of content is in some sense psychological, it has an unavoidable social dimension.

The ontological claims of methodological individualism, namely, that mental phenomena are individual entities, are seriously shaken, whatever the type of (social) explanation prescribed. Here one might be tempted to think that the problem becomes particularly acute in Boudon's approach, if not because he presents contrasting accounts of causal explanation (one requires the instant production of a law, and the other, merely the existence of a law under a particular description), then because he lacks a concept of causality which refers to sub- and supra-intentional phenomena. In fact, it can be shown that both approaches are haunted by the same ghost: Humean causal laws. As we have seen in the previous section, one of the main problems relating to the causal status of macro-social entities refers to the absence of general and universal Humean laws in social phenomena. This leads Boudon to relativise their role in explanation by differentiating descriptive from causal laws. The former, described in terms of a functional explanation, assume an equivalent role to Elster's 'hermeneutic method' or to Davidson's theory of interpretation. Causal laws, on the other hand, are accounted for in terms of Davidson's statement that reasons can be causes; nonetheless, differently from Elster and Davidson, Boudon believes that *reasons have to synthesise social and psychological data* (Boudon, 1995a: 552). That this requirement only pushes further away the determination of causality, leaving unresolved the problem of social causes, can be shown with Bhaskar's critique of Davidson's analysis of singular causal statements.

Singular causal statements are analysed as follows: '"A caused B" is true if and only if there are descriptions of A and B such that the sentences obtained by putting these descriptions for "A" and "B" in "A caused B" follows from a true causal law' (Davidson *apud* Bhaskar, 1997: 140). For Bhaskar, this suggestion places an impossible, useless and unnecessary requirement on the verification of causal claims. It is impossible because the original causal claim is presumably only made insofar as we do not have the complete state-descriptions representing the antecedents and consequents which 'A' and 'B' represent. Although Davidson argues that such claims can be defended by producing a relevant (neurological, chemical or physical) law, or by giving reasons for believing such a law exists, this may render the causal claim useless insofar as it does not allow us to discriminate between true and false causal claims at the level concerned: 'neurological laws are consistent with any social event and so cannot be possibly used to defend specific causal claims involving people' (Bhaskar, 1997: 141). In addition to that, the recourse to a Humean causal law to cover particular cases rests on regularity determinism, i.e. on the belief in the philosophical dogma according to which the principle 'same cause, same effect', everywhere applies. To the extent that causal claims can be better defended by an appeal to the normic statements concerning the level at which the original causal claim was made, Davidson's idea that causal claims entail Humean laws is also unnecessary.

Contrary to the ontology of events which inspires Davidson's account of laws, an ontology of structures leads to a conception of law as normic statements that refer to the exercise of tendencies or causal powers which may not be manifested. In this sense, they do not describe the patterns of events which we observe in the world in general and in our everyday actions. Events are not described by any laws of Nature, and not even governed by them, for:

> Laws do not describe the patterns or legitimate the prediction of kinds of events. Rather it seems they must be conceived, at least as regards the ordinary things of the world, as situating the limits and imposing constraints on the types of action possible for a given kind of thing. Laws then not only predicate tendencies (which when exercised constitute the normic behaviour) or novel kinds (or of familiar things in novel or limit situations); they impose (more or less absolute) constraints on familiar things. ... Laws ascribe possibilities which may not be realized and impose necessities which constrain but do not determine; they ascribe the former to novel kinds and impose the latter on familiar things.
>
> (Bhaskar, 1997: 105–6)

The idea is, generally speaking, that science has to deal with causal explanation in a double way: first, it has to explain the causal properties of agents following from their internal structure; in addition to that, it has to 'explain the occurrence of particular events in terms of conjunctures of the causal properties of various interacting mechanisms' (Porpora, 1998: 343). For this reason, causal laws are not deterministic, but contingent, though typically universal, in the sense that they apply to all objects of a certain kind; and this is also why they can be conceived as 'normic statements', i.e. statements that, while referring to some sort of generalisation, do allow for exceptions. It follows from this perspective that the generalities of social life must not be regarded as the result of deterministic laws that strictly govern the relations between its elements, but as the result of the (inter-) action of the causal powers which are inherent to different types of agents (human agents and social structures). This renders Boudon's differentiation between causal statements and descriptive laws rather vacuous.

That reasons can be causes can thus be defended by reference to the causal powers and liabilities of human agents. Nonetheless, their causal powers and liabilities cannot be accounted for solely in terms of individual mental contents, particularly if these causal powers and liabilities are conceived as cognitive capacities which are socially constructed. Although it is possible to treat these as given, in the sense of independent variables, the theory of cognitive rationality has, if it wants to account for belief and preference formation, to relate them to social conditions. These conditions impose themselves upon individuals and their mental contents in a causal (though non-deterministic) manner. In this sense, Boudon (1996c) is essentially correct when he differentiates the social from the psychological individual, characterising the former mainly in terms of the position he/she occupies in the social structure, the roles attached to these positions, and some individual variations in the way these roles are performed. He is also correct when he states that it is often possible to explain social phenomena by reference to the (good) reasons which led to action. His mistake is to conclude from that the possibility of reducing statements about the social structure to statements about the individual, to reduce social to individual mechanisms through an appeal to some idea of 'final', 'rock-bottom' or 'white-box' explanation (Boudon, 1998). To the extent that this idea prevents any account of both belief and preference formation, one of the main aims of the theory of cognitive rationality, i.e. the explanation of the adherence to false positive and normative beliefs based on the (often socially constructed) dispositions of individuals who are placed in particular social contexts becomes impossible to attain. It also prevents the use of a coherent causal criterion to establish the reality of the social structures, thus of a reality which is more or less independent of agents' conceptions. This, in its turn, renders impossible the distinction between true and false beliefs given the lack of objective criteria for accessing agents' conceptions of reality.

Concluding remarks

I have tried to establish here the main characteristics of Boudon's neo-Weberian explanation through a comparison with what Boudon takes to be the two principal alternatives in social theory: the neo-Durkheimian and interpretative paradigms. Boudon's neo-Weberianism can be understood as a naturalistic paradigm, in the sense that it takes the method of the social sciences to be fundamentally the same as the method of the natural sciences, and claims that both groups of sciences should aim at objectivity. Nonetheless, in comparison with the natural sciences, the social sciences present some specific characteristics, namely the fact that it is not only possible, but sometimes imperative that the social analyst interpret his or her data with the aid of some commonsense knowledge which is based on social experience. This idea is expressed in the principle of *Verstehen*, which is not considered by Boudon as an alternative to explanation as it applies to the natural sciences, but as a form of explanation that applies to human action.

Understanding is differentiated from interpretation according to the levels of reality to which they apply (individual actions and collective phenomena respectively), and understanding is considered to present, at least in principle, a higher degree of objectivity than interpretation, because it relates to causal explanation in a much more direct way than interpretation, thus allowing for the verification of causal claims. Whereas understanding deals with the reasons an individual had for acting (or not acting) in a given situation, interpretation (especially hermeneutic interpretation) deals with the possible significance a given social system, rules, norms, etc., may have for both the analyst and the individuals involved.

The particular importance interpretation assumes in the neo-Weberian paradigm resides in the idea that every statement about reality has to be judged according to general symbolic frameworks. Boudon considers these frameworks to be so fundamental to both commonsense and scientific knowledge that it is often impossible to detach the notion of truth from the language which arises from a particular framework. For this reason, he believes that truth cannot be considered unique: sometimes it can be considered as such, other times it cannot, depending on both the nature of the object in question and the quality of the competing models used to explain that object.

The existence of situations of multiple truth, here understood in the specific sense of situations in which it is impossible to determine what is the correct explanation or description of a particular object of knowledge, justifies, in Boudon's view, putting aside explanatory aims in favour of interpretation. Interpretation can be either a temporary or a final aim, depending on what it aims at clarifying.

Because Boudon considers the notion of cause as particularly obscure, interpretation can simply precede causal explanation (instead of replacing it) and, in this sense, it is considered to be a condition of intelligibility in social explanation. This kind of interpretation does not necessarily assume a hermeneutical character: all kinds of structural analysis are taken to be based on descriptive laws which have an interpretative but not necessarily hermeneutical status.

Boudon's differentiation between causal and descriptive laws and his denial that the former exist in social reality makes his notion of cause much less ambiguous when it refers to individual causes, i.e. when it refers to reasons, rather than when it refers to collective entities. The nomological conception of explanation provides, according to Boudon, a weak notion of causality for the social sciences because the empirical regularities observed at the macroscopic levels are taken to be the effects of actions rather than the expressions of laws or rules which can structure reality (Boudon, 1986b: 875).

Given the contingent character of structural regularities, Boudon postulates a difference between causal and descriptive laws and conceives social mechanisms solely in terms of a set of causal statements situated at the agency level (Boudon, 1998). However, as I have attempted to demonstrate here, the conception of causality based on descriptive laws which is applied to the structural level does not solve the problem of the causal links between social structures and reasons (particularly good reasons). Although it is not a matter of denying the importance of explanation based on reasons, the theory of cognitive rationality itself points to the need to explain the more or less necessary existence of false, socially grounded, beliefs. In other words, one has to account for the causal powers of the social structure in the characterisation of a social agent: an agent which is more or less constrained by his/her position in the social structure and by the roles which inform his/her dispositions to act in certain ways and to believe in certain things.

An explanation through the reasons of an agent defined in the way described above represents an important social mechanism. Its explanatory power springs from the fact that reasons refer to the intrinsic power of actors to, given the appropriate circumstances, bring about particular states of affairs. In this sense, Boudon subscribes to the rationalist postulate shared by authors such as James Coleman or Martin Hollis, according to which 'when a sociological phenomenon is made the outcome of individual reasons, one does not need to ask further questions' (Boudon, 1998). It was seen, however, that Boudon does not always consider the intrinsic character of causes (or the necessary relations between a cause and its effects) and, to the extent that he also subscribes to Donald Davidson's modified Humean account of causality, explanation through reasons also presents its own drawbacks. According to this latter approach, reasons merely represent a particular formulation of some type of unknown cause which has to be accounted for in terms of a general law. This law is, in its turn, characterised in terms of event regularity and can never be formulated at the level of reasons, but presupposes some form of reductionism (to singular physical, neurological, etc., events).

Reasons are a type of cause, but, as with structural causes, they cannot be reduced to events: they refer to underlying states or dispositions which are inherent to agents. This account of reason explanation is not compatible with the Humean definition of cause and causal laws described by Davidson, and Boudon does not seem to be aware of this incompatibility. Although actions can be often described in terms of events, differently from actions, 'reasons are possessed even when unexercised, and only exercised under suitable conditions' (Bhaskar, 1979: 119). For this reason, an actualist ontology which reduces reality to either empirical phenomena or to events is not compatible with explanation through reasons.

The actualist ontology which informs Boudon's methodological positions also has consequences for his anti-relativistic claims. The impossibility of establishing the reality of a non-empirical object such as the social structure makes it particularly difficult for Boudon to judge theories based on different languages: it is only if we accept the existence of an objective reality, relatively independent of our descriptions of it, that one can have a basis for comparing and evaluating different theories. In particular, the critique of the lack of objectivity of the hermeneutic tradition has to rest on the possibility of showing that the agents' account of their situation can be mistaken, in the sense that a certain set of categories and concepts are not applicable to experience. Such a critique is important for Boudon's theory of cognitive rationality to the extent that it can establish that even though a belief may be real, thus having an important explanatory role, the entities described in the belief may not be real insofar as they are neither empirically observable, nor can their causal powers or tendencies be shown to exist. This means that social science has a particularly important role not only in showing that some beliefs may not correspond to reality, but also in establishing the social conditions which led to those false beliefs, thus justifying its normative dimension.

The arguments developed in this chapter can be summarised as an attempt to show the importance of a robust conception of causality to the establishment of non-empirical criteria of theory testing and concept building. The lack of such a conception bears important consequences for the notion of objectivity to the extent that it does not allow us to differentiate reality from the language used to describe it, thus leaving the social analyst with two equally problematic alternatives: a linguistic realism or essentialism which equates reality with the concepts employed by science, or a nominalist perspective which renders impossible the establishment of rational criteria for the choice between alternative concepts and theoretical frameworks.

5   Conclusion

The methodological reflections or the 'critical attitude' which provide a basis for Boudon's substantive work represent, to a large extent, his concern with the relation between empirical and conceptual activity. His critique is, however, limited by the central or exclusive role accorded to epistemological issues to the detriment of ontological ones. This generates the paradoxical view described by Outhwaite (1987: 19) as 'the apparently robust epistemologies which allow us to be certain about our experiences but not that of which they are experiences (the external world, other minds, or even our own bodies)'.

As realist philosophers of science have argued, any serious theory of knowledge has to be based on a commonsense ontology which takes for granted the existence of the world. Moreover, if we assume at the outset that social theory should be concerned with the characterisation of social objects and processes, then it becomes clear that, whether or not we decide to cross the academic frontier between philosophy and the social sciences, theoretical activity presents an ontological dimension which cannot be brushed aside.

That every knowledge presupposes and/or generates an ontology is not difficult to establish. What I can know of a particular object depends, to a large extent, on what I take that object to be. The problem arises when being is reduced to knowledge about being, particularly to knowledge based on experience. To use a favourite realist quote, 'to be is more than to be perceived', and it is possible to know that something exists without being able to determine what it is exactly. Knowledge of such things is made possible by transcendental arguments, and this is one of the possible ways of linking philosophical or conceptual reflection with some empirical science.

Most objects dealt with by the social sciences do not present direct empirical referents which can justify their existence. However, non-empirical objects, such as society itself, are often deemed to have a real existence to the extent that they are taken to be possible objects of an empirical science. The question thus becomes that of reconciling the existence of such objects with epistemological positions which do not authorise us to make any assumptions beyond that which is either immediately given to our senses, or actually determined.

This problem is particularly relevant to the understanding of Boudon's paradigm of social action. On the one hand, it is conceived as a *social* paradigm, that is, as a framework which enables us to understand concrete social phenomena. On the other, it assumes that social phenomena can only be properly accounted for in terms of their 'most basic' elements, i.e. individual actions, given that the former cannot exist without the latter. Although Boudon insists on the fact that methodological individualism does not rest on any ontological assumptions about the (non-) reality of social structures, its epistemological justification generates a social nominalism which is more or less evident throughout his work. Given the implicit character of this relation between a given epistemological and methodological perspective, on the one hand, and a particular social ontology, on the other, a philosophically oriented reflection, such as the one provided by critical realists, can be very useful.

The main thrust of the philosophically oriented critique developed here lies in demonstrating that an individualistic approach generates some insurmountable problems for an adequate account of social phenomena, particularly if this account rests on a model such as Boudon's model of cognitive rationality. In fact, the more Boudon distances himself from a narrow definition of rationality, the more he has to distance himself from methodological individualism because the model of actor which he advocates requires a strong account of his/her location within the social structure and the effects he/she is bound to suffer and to produce. In this sense, the understanding of both subjective and objective meaning involves some sort of reference to the social structures, and this cannot be done purely in terms of individual mental contents.

As was seen in Chapter 1, one of the bases for the denial of ontological individualism lies in the adoption of a nominalist approach, loosely defined as the idea that sociological concepts and theories should be understood as 'models' which bear a more or less adequate relation to reality, but never a relation of strict correspondence. Strictly speaking, that does not constitute a *social* nominalism, but merely an anti-essentialist approach which aims at differentiating models, concepts and theories from reality. With this type of argument, Boudon aims to demonstrate that there is no ontological justification for methodological individualism because nominalism applies to concepts relating to both the structure and the agency level.

The problem with this argument, which identifies realism and essentialism, lies in how to account for the relations between scientific concepts and models, on the one hand, and reality, on the other, if there are no ontological considerations at stake. It is my position here that Boudon is able to establish the adequacy of concepts and models relating to the level of agency in a much more coherent way than of those relating to social structures, even though he does not explore the full consequences of this in terms of an ontology of the social actor. As a result, there is a difference in the role that each type of entity (individual agents and social structures) plays in social explanation to the extent that the individual level of analysis is in fact compatible with a non-empiricist ontology. This makes it possible for him to include non-empirical elements, such as reasons, in his explanation of actions in a rather unproblematic way.

The compatibility between explanation through reasons and a non-empiricist ontology springs directly from a rationalist epistemology according to which human reasons are true a priori notions, in the specific sense that actions are always generated by them or, in other words, that reasons are a necessary (logical) condition for the existence of actions and of an individual self. What we have here is a rationalist causal criterion for the ascription of the reality of certain mental contents which assume the form of reasons. This epistemology has, however, close affinities with an individualist ontology to the extent that the conceptual or rational aspects of social phenomena are also emphasised, generating a conception of social structure merely in terms of conceptual constructs which are present in the minds of agents and social researchers.

For Boudon, mental contents, particularly reasons, are established with the aid of hypotheses which are then confirmed through the effects they generate as a result of their being treated as causally efficacious forces. Reasons are considered to be truly a priori in the sense that they are necessary mechanisms of social action, but their content can only be established a posteriori, i.e. according to the social situation in which they develop. This is where Boudon's approach distances itself from a strong form of rationalism according to which real definitions can be achieved solely in terms of logical or conceptual necessities.

The causal efficacy of reasons is more evident the more they relate to the ideal type of instrumental rational action, since this ideal type represents the greater degree of individual freedom from external influences. This freedom, as I have argued in Chapter 2, is always taken to exist in social life, albeit in different degrees. This accounts for an implicit definition of the human individual as a causal agent who has the capability of doing things, making it possible to conceive an ontology of the individual in terms of a real object which presents a greater or lesser degree of rationality and freedom, or, using a realist language foreign to Boudon, in terms of his or her causal powers, dispositions or tendencies to act in a certain way. Because actors are not completely free from external influences, this does not mean that their powers are exercised in all circumstances, but only given the appropriate (including structural) conditions.

Given the ambiguous nature which Boudon attributes to the notion of cause in the social sciences, this realist conception of the social actor is only sustained in a partially unconscious and contradictory manner. The contradictory character of his ontology of the social actor can be observed through his claim to have adopted Donald Davidson's account of reasons as causes, as described in Chapter 4: an actualist approach according to which causes do not refer to the intrinsic powers or tendencies of things, but to the constant conjunction of events which ground Humean laws, even if in a rather modified form.

Collective objects, in their turn, are taken to exist only by virtue of their being conceptually present in the minds of individuals, and their reality as independent objects could only be proven if similar causal powers could be attributed to them. This possibility is in fact considered by Boudon in his critique of empiricism: scientific models can be judged adequate if the 'forces' they represent can be proven to exist and act in the way the model describes. Huygens's theory of the pendulum (one of Boudon's favourite examples to illustrate this fact) postulates the existence of causal forces which describe the movement of a pendulum, even though these forces cannot be directly observed.

Notwithstanding that, the epistemological justification for methodological individualism cannot generate an ontology compatible with realism at the structural level, because there is neither an a priori (conceptual) nor an a posteriori (material) cause which accounts for those objects as the bearers of certain causal powers, that is, in terms of agents. Nonetheless, the nominalist character of social structures is not always sustained by Boudon. Chapter 2 constitutes the attempt to show that, although the explanatory role attributed to the notion of structure varies according to the phase of his substantive work, it always assumes a 'residual role' in the explanation of social phenomena. This could mean that social structures are deemed a 'real existence' insofar as they are the causes of mental phenomena, that is, their existence is ascertained in explanatory terms. It was shown, however, that the explanatory role of the social structures is minimised through a recourse to what Boudon calls 'methodological determinism', i.e. the idea that the causal role attributed to social structures constitutes merely a heuristic device, justified in terms of the impossibility of their *ad infinitum* reduction to individual actions.

This position is also not easily or coherently sustained: in order to avoid the atomistic implications of a model of an actor conceived in terms of *Homo economicus*, Boudon tries to develop a conception of an actor which represents a synthesis between the latter and the socially determined *Homo sociologicus*. This synthesis, examined in Chapter 3, is expressed in terms of a rational agent whose rationality is bounded by his or her social situation. The social situation of actors relates to the structural and conjunctural elements which account for the objective constraints and for enabling conditions of their actions and, in particular, to the cognitive skills and motivations which are at the root of their reasons. In this sense, one of the main advantages of this model of an actor refers to the social dimension of the actors described by sociology, in opposition to both an abstract universal subject and a psychological agent.

The theory of cognitive rationality developed from this model can be characterised as the attempt to do away with social determinism, utilitarianism and relativism by explaining social phenomena in terms of the 'good reasons' which lead to action. Good reasons, contrary to a thin definition of rationality, are intrinsically linked to a social context, and are neither necessarily objectively valid nor merely the result of the idiosyncrasies of individuals. However, given the lack of a conception of social structure as a reality in its own right which can be reduced neither to individual mental contents nor to the unintended consequences of the actions of the individuals 'here and now present', the main problem which can be identified in this theory (or rather in the paradigm of action which informs it) refers to the impossibility of differentiating good reasons which are not objectively valid from good reasons which are objectively valid, thus opening up the possibility of an ontological relativism to which Boudon does not subscribe.

It becomes evident that Boudon needs a strong conception of social structure both in order to account for the socially grounded character of reasons, and to be able to differentiate reality from the agents' conceptions of it. And given the non-empirical character of the social structure, it becomes particularly important to ground this conception in a robust theory of causality which rests, in its turn, on a realist ontology.

According to this ontology, reality can be reduced neither to empirical phenomena nor to its actual manifestations. Apart from those two levels (the empirical and the actual, which refer to experiences and events respectively), it also includes the level of generative mechanisms which may or may not generate events and allow for experiences. This is intrinsically related to the idea that causal laws refer to some 'generative mechanisms' of Nature, a realist metaphor for denoting the particular ways of acting of objects which continue to be potentially operative even when not actually manifest. Because these generative mechanisms are often 'out of phase' with actual patterns of events, a constant conjunction of events is neither a necessary nor a sufficient condition for the identification of a law.

The realist critique of the Humean conception of causality and of the different forms of actualism which ground it constitutes, in my view, one of the most coherent approaches to the (non-deterministic) relation between structure and agency in the social sciences. To the extent that it accounts for the necessary powers of both types of agents and the way they affect each other (including the possibility of one tendency being neutralised by another), the notion of necessity which allows for the differentiation between causal and spurious relations can be maintained, without the need to assume that this necessity is deterministic in any actual sense.

The adoption of such an ontology of structures, meaning that the world is both structured and stratified, allows for different levels of explanation without having to reduce one level of reality to another, a reduction which often allows for 'half-explanations' based on the higher stratum, as is the case with methodological individualism.

The notion of social structure which derives from a realist ontology such as the one described above can be conceived of as a metaphor, 'a causal mechanism constituted by the relationships among social positions that accounts for social phenomena in terms of tendencies, strains and forces inherent in the nexus of those relationships' (Porpora, 1998: 340). This conception, while pointing to the structure's ontological dependency on agents (the actual occupants of positions), does not imply that it is possible, or even desirable, that structures are dissolved into the agency level. On the contrary, the idea is that it is necessary to relate the tendencies and dispositions inherent to both the social structure and the social actors in order to account for the reproduction and transformation of societies.

It is only to the extent that one takes for granted the existence of some social objects, establishing, at the same time, that they can be real because their reality can be accounted for either in empirical or in causal terms, that the social sciences can exist at all. As Durkheim tried to show throughout his work, it is only because there is an object called society which is relatively opaque to spontaneous understanding and which cannot be accounted for by any other branch of knowledge, that sociology has its *raison d'être*, being both possible and necessary. In this sense, and contrary to some of Durkheim's methodological prescriptions, it is important to deal with non-empirical phenomena which, despite the somewhat tentative character of our definitions, can be established as real emergent properties because they present some inherent and non-reducible causal powers, tendencies and liabilities.

Of course the inclusion of such objects in the theory of cognitive rationality involves not only a different account of causality, but also a rejection of its individualistic basis. However, as I have tried to demonstrate throughout this book, it is only under these conditions that Boudon can seriously speak of social structures as both the causes and effects of mental phenomena. And it is only on this condition that the theory of cognitive rationality presents some advantage over those models and theories which, through relying on a narrow definition of rationality, are both less general and less realistic than the former. In a nutshell, critical realism, because it represents a non-actualist ontology which entails the rejection of both a Humean account of causality and of methodological individualism, can provide a stronger basis for Boudon's theory of cognitive rationality.

Notes

1 The action paradigm: bringing the agent back in

1 Determinism is taken in the very particular sense of explanation solely in terms of elements prior to the action in question. In this sense, if an actor is placed in a situation where he/she is forced to choose, Boudon still considers this kind of explanation as belonging to interactionist paradigms, even though the explanation may be deterministic in the usual sense. This idea is expressed by Giddens in terms of *agent causality*, according to which 'action is caused by an agent's reflexive monitoring of his or her intentions in relation to both wants and appreciation of the demands of the "outer" world', and *event causality*. For Giddens, as for Boudon, 'determinism, in the social sciences, then refers to any theoretical scheme which reduces human action solely to "event causality"' (Giddens, 1993: 91–2).

2 The concept of state of nature is the equivalent of what Boudon calls 'systems of interdependence', i.e. 'systems of interaction where individual actions can be analysed without reference to the category of roles' (Boudon, 1981: 255).

3 'M est une fonction M (m_i, m_j) des comportements m_i des acteurs de categorie i et de comportements m_j des acteurs j (à suposer qu'on doive effectivement distinguer dans le probléme sus examen les deux catégories sociales i et j); M = M (m_i, m_j)'. 'En résumé, il faut faire du comportement m_i une fonction de la Situation S_i e de m_j une fonction de S_j: $m_i = m_i (S_i)$ et $m_j = m_j (S_j)$'.

4 'On ne considérera pas les individus effectivement responsables de M dans leur individualité concrète, mais on les classera en grandes catégories. On ne considérera pas tous les traits du système social, mais seulement le petit nombre de traits P qui paraissent suffire à l'explication. Bref, on construit un modèle extrêmement simplificateur pour expliquer une réalité généralement complexe.'

5 'Pour expliquer un phénomène social … il est indispensable de reconstruire les motivations des individus concernés par le phénomène en question, et d'appréhender ce phénomène comme le résultat de l'agrégation des comportements individuels dictés par ces motivations.'

6 'On verra que la définition donnée du concept d'attitude ne se preoccupe guère de correspondre à la notion courante du terme; elle aboutit plutôt à identifier, au niveau du langage de la recherche, un objet scientifique

particulier, muni d'un certain nombre de caractères (inobservabilité, polarité ...). Là est bien l'essentiel: l'observabilité implique des techniques d'inférence spéciales, l'intentionalité suppose un stimulus verbal ou réel, etc., de sorte que sous le terme d'attitude, c'est un démarche spécifique de la recherche qui est identifiée. Le non lui-même importe peu: "disposition", "sentiment", seraient aussi justifiés.'

7 'Postulat 1: les phénomenes sociaux sont le produit d'actions, d'attitudes, de croyances individuelles; ils résultent de leur agregation. ...

Postulat 2: expliquer ces actions, attitudes, croyances, c'est les tendre compréhensibles. C'est-à-dire que le sociologue doit retrouver le sense de ces actions, de ces croyances ou de ces attitudes pour l'acteur social lui-même. Plus précisément, car la notion de sens n'est pas d'une clarté parfaite, le sociologue doit retrouver les raisons qui font que l'acteur fait (ou a fait) X, croit (ou a cru) que Y est vrai ou bon, etc.'

8 According to Martin Hollis (1977: 143ff.), rationalism has three distinct senses. First, there is a sense in which rationalism is identified with the very broad belief that there is some order in experience which makes science possible. This is not incompatible with empiricism, for it merely ascertains that Nature is a rational system of causes and effects, governed by laws which can be discovered by Reason. Another sense of the word is identified with those theories of human action which assume rationality in human beings, such as the one developed by Boudon. A third sense of the word refers to the philosophical opposition to empiricism, which, in broad terms, states that 'Reason is the power of the mind to penetrate the veil of perception' (Hollis, 1994: 545). In its stronger version, represented here by the latter definition, causal laws are viewed in terms of intrinsic or necessary (logical) relations between a cause and its effects.

9 'T' stands for a theory, 'T', and 'q' for a logical deduction, 'q'.

10 Boudon develops the following model of subjective probability: 'Let us call P_1 the likelihood that the consequences of a theory T_1 may be drawn from an alternative theory T_1'. Then $1 - P$ would represent the likelihood that the consequences of a theory T_1 may not drawn from an alternative theory T_1'. What our previous assumption amounts saying is then that $1 - P$ is an increasing function of the number of independent consequences which may be drawn from a theory T_x. Let us call N_x this number and let f be an increasing function; we have then: $1 - P_x = f(N_x)$. As regards the quantity $1 - P_x$, it measures the likelihood that the set of consequences $\{C_x\}$ could not be drawn from a theory other than T_x. If we suppose $1 - P_x = 1$, this would mean that $\{C_x\}$ could not be drawn from a theory which would be distinct from T_x. In that case, T_x would be not only *not false* but also *true*. In other words, $1 - P_x$ may be conceived as representing the likelihood for T_x to be *true*' (Boudon, 1972: 413–14).

11 This emphasis on subjective meaning rests on the assumption that meaning is an individual mental state. According to Enzo Di Nuoscio (1993: 16–17), for example, both Boudon and Weber state that it is only possible to understand and explain actions by placing oneself in the agents' shoes and, in addition to that, meaningful action can only be attributed to individual

persons. In this sense, the method called *Verstehen* only makes sense if one is dealing with individual actors, who are the only ones to which mental states can be attributed.

12 '[L]a *vérification* de l'analyse peut se situer et a avantage à se situer à deux niveaux: *au niveaux m*, celui de la compréhension: on cherchera, si cela est possible, à vérifier que les mécanismes psychologiques postulés par l'observateur informé des données principales de la situation S correspondent à la réalité. *Au niveau M*: on vérifiera que les conséquences au niveau agrégé des hypothèses microsociologiques m sont bien conformes aux données agrégées telles qu'elles sont empiriquement observées.'

13 '[L]a "perspective" très générale qui consiste à concevoir l'objet qu'on se propose d'analyser comme un tout, comme un ensemble d'eléments interdépendents don il s'agit de démontrer la cohérence'.

2 Linking structure and agency in Boudon's substantive analyses

1 I largely owe this classification to Dr Alban Bouvier.

2 'My primary objective is to attempt to explain why the tremendous educational development that occurred in all Western societies following World War II has had so little impact on equality; that is, why IEO (inequality of educational opportunities) has decreased so little and why ISO (inequality of social opportunities), in spite of this development, does not appear to have decreased at all.' (Boudon, 1974: XV).

3 In the second part of *Education, Opportunity, and Social Inequality*, Boudon compares the paradoxes of education with similar problems from economic theory (every individual has an advantage in obtaining as much education as possible, but the aggregation of these individual actions results in the degeneration of the expectation associated with most educational levels). For a critique of the economic concepts employed in this comparison and the applicability of game theory to the aforementioned paradox see Jon Elster (1976).

4 Although the English version of *The Unintended Consequences of Social Action* dates from 1982, the original French version (*Effets Pervers et Ordre Social*) dates from 1977. Moreover, this book is a collection of articles which, for the most part, were published before the book.

5 'The image of a "rational" *homo sociologicus* is not implied in the perverse effect paradigm, but the image of an "intentional" one is.' (Boudon, 1982: 7). The intentional *homo sociologicus* is defined as 'an intentional actor, endowed with a set of preferences, seeking acceptable ways of realising his objectives, more or less conscious of the degree of control he has over the elements of the situation in which he finds himself (conscious, in other words, of the structural constraints that limit his possibilities of action), acting in the light of limited information and in a situation of uncertainty. In short, the key feature of the concept of *homo sociologicus* used here is *limited rationality*.' (ibid.: 9).

6 '[A]nalyser l'adhésion du sujet social à une idée non fondée objectivement, c'est comprendre le sens qu'elle a pour lui. En termes plus clairs, c'est mettre en évidence les raisons qu'il a de l'adopter.'

7 'Il est évident que ce que je vois ici et maintenant dépend de ma localisation dans l'espace. On ne voit pas la même chose du côté cour et du côté jardin, et ce que je vois du côté cour dépend notamment de ce que je sais déja, comme le fait qu'une charmante voisine ou qu'un couple acariâtre réside dans l'appartement d'en face.'

8 'Le mot dispositions sont donc les resources cognitives, les savoirs que nous avons acquis et que nous pouvons mobiliser.'

9 'Le sociologue peut considérer les acteurs sociaux comme rationnels. Il a même avantage à le faire, si l'on croit Max Weber. Mais, en même temps, il doit tirer toutes les conséquences du fait que les acteurs sociaux sont socialement situés, c'est-à-dire qu'ils tiennent des rôles sociaux, qu'ils appartiennent à certains milieux sociaux et à certaines sociétés, qu'ils disposent de certaines ressources (notamment cognitives), et qu'en raison des processus de socialisation auxquels ils on été exposés, ils ont intériorisé un certain nombre de savoirs et de représentations. Pour ces raisons, ils sont sujets à ce que j'ai appelé des effets de situation (effets de position e de disposition).'

10 '... je ne tire en aucune façon la conclusion que toutes les croyances doivent s'expliquer par des raisons. ... il est vrai que bien des croyances on des causes affectives, que celles-ci soient ou non observables.'

11 Boudon defines belief as the adoption of 'doubtful, fragile or false ideas': 'To the classical definition belicf = für wahr halten (consider something as true), I add the condition that what we take to be true is either not true or not assured enough.' In the original, 'A la définition classique croire = für wahr halten (tenir pour vrai), j'ajoute donc la condition que ce qu'on tient pour tel ne l'est pas ou est peu assuré.' (Boudon, 1990a: 15).

12 '... une argumentation parfaitement valide peut conduire à des idées fausses, dans la mesure où nous ne percevons pas les propositions implicites qui l'environnent et où nous ne prenons pas conscience du fait que nos conclusions dérivent aussi de ces propositions implicites que nous adoptons tacitement parce que nous avons de bonnes raisons de les adopter.'

13 'Comme le sociologue s'intéresse aux croyances collectives, il faut préciser que ce sens subjectif tend a être partagé par tous ceux qui se trouvent dans la même situation.'

14 Although Boudon has changed the expression 'subjective rationality' to 'cognitive rationality', this does not imply any change in its content: 'In previous publications, I have used the expression "subjective rationality" instead of what I call here "cognitive rationality". I have borrowed the notion of "subjective rationality from H. Simon. It seems to me, today, that (such as with the synonymic notion of "limited rationality") it bears an intrinsic negative connotation. The expression "cognitive rationality" presents the advantage of indicating that such rationality is present within normal processes of knowledge production. On the other hand, it avoids the utopian evocation of an "unlimited rationality"'. 'Dans des publications antérieures, j'avais utilisé l'expression de "rationalité subjective" en lieu et place de ce que j'appelle ici la "rationalité cognitive". J'avais empruté la

notion de "rationalité subjective" a H. Simon. Elle me paraît aujourd'hui (comme la notion synonyme de "rationalité limitée") comporter une connotation négative gênante. L'expression de "rationalité cognitive" a l'avantage d'indiquer que ladite rationalité est presénte derrière les processus normaux de production de la connaissance. Elle évite en outre d'evoquer l'utopie d'une "rationalité illimitée."' (Boudon, 1995a: 105–6).

15 'Il n'est pas non plus question de nier que, dans la plupart de cas, éléments affectifs et éléments rationnels se melent indissociablement. Le sentiment d'indignation qu'on éprouve lorsqu'une personne affaiblie par l'âge es soulagée de ses ressources par un proche indélicat se fonde sur de raisons universelles. C'est parce que ce sentiment s'appuie sur des raisons immédiatement compréhensibles par quiconque qu'il est vécu de façon vive sur le plan affectif. Même lorsque ces raisons ne sont qu'imparfaitement conscients chez le sujet, ce son bien elles que sont la cause de la réaction et du sentiment qu'il éprouve.'

16 '[L]es horreurs de la seconde Guerre mondiale avaient engendré un consensus sur les valeurs démocratiques, tandis que les tensions de la guerre froid provoquaient un effet de rassemblement autour des valeurs fondatrices de la nation américaine'.

17 'parce qu'elle est contrariée par la présence de facteurs particuliers.'

3 Beyond *Homo sociologicus* and *Homo economicus:* a complex theory of rationality

1 Bentham and Mill's basic formulation, known as act-utilitarianism, states that an act is right if it produces good consequences (at least as good as any other alternative in terms of welfare). (Frey, 1994). The keynote to Bentham's philosophy can be found in his *Introduction to the Principles of Morals and Legislation*: 'Nature has placed man under the governance of two sovereign masters, *pain* and *pleasure*. It is for them alone to point out what we ought to do, as well as to determine what we shall do. On the one hand the standard of right and wrong, on the other the chain of causes and effects, are fastened to their throne. ... The *principle of utility* recognizes this subjection, and assumes it for the foundation of that system, the object of which is to rear the fabric of felicity by the hands of reason and of law' (Bentham *apud* Davidson, 1957: 28). James Mill also subscribed to the idea that pleasure and pain are the essence of morality and that, being intrinsically rational, human beings have the power of appreciating the consequences of their actions in the light of an addition or diminution of the sum of pleasures (utility) (ibid.).

2 Boudon makes the same point in relation to Rousseau and Adam Smith. From this, he concludes that both Durkheim and Parsons had a view of the utilitarian tradition which was never in accordance with historical reality (Boudon, 1989a).

3 This does not imply a necessary relation between anti-utilitarianism and sociologism.

4   'Dans la conception classique, l'acte irrationnel (p.e. l'acte impulsif inspiré
    par la colère) est à la fois plus ou moins conscient et plus ou moins
    transparent: je sais que j'ai agi par colère, et les autres peuvent la percevoir
    de leur côté. Ici, la motivation irrationelle est donc facilement confirmée à
    la fois par l'expérience interne et par l'observation externe. Il en va tout
    autrement dans le cas des actes irrationnels au sens moderne: ici, la
    motivation irrationnelle est un construit inaccessible et à l'experience interne
    et à l'observation externe. Ainsi, l'"instinct d'imitation" (Tarde), le "désir
    mimétique" (R. Girard), la "résistance au changement" (Var. Auct.),
    l'"aveuglement par l'intêt" (K. Marx), les "pulsions inconscientes" du
    premier Freud, la "fausse conscience" (F. Mehring, F. Engels) ne peuvent
    être ni vécus, ni observés, mais seulement inférés. De telles notions soulèvent
    de graves difficultés méthodologiques, psychologiques et sociologiques'.

5   Here it becomes clear that Boudon extends the realm of action in order to
    include those kinds of behaviour which are unintended but meaningful
    (inspired by reasons). The same cannot be said of some rational-choice
    theories, whose very existence depends on the intentional and goal-oriented
    character of behaviour. In this sense, beliefs are only considered to the extent
    that they are reasons for the behaviour to be explained, nothing being said
    about the reasons for the adoption of these beliefs. In other words, beliefs
    are treated as mere data.

6   The differences between value-oriented and affective action is put by Weber
    in the following terms: 'the orientation of value-rational action is
    distinguished from the affectual type by its clearly self-conscious formulation
    of the ultimate values governing the action and the consistently planned
    orientation of its detailed course to these values. ... Action is affectual if it
    satisfies a need for revenge, sensual gratification, devotion, contemplative
    bliss, or for working off emotional tensions (irrespective of the level of
    sublimation)' (Weber, 1978: 25). Although it can be argued that all Weberian
    types of social action relate to rationality, Weber does not include affective
    actions in the realm of value-rationality. Boudon's interpretation seems to
    be closer to Habermas (1996: 336): 'When we examine moral disagreements,
    we must include affective reactions in the class of moral utterances. ... The
    critical and self-critical stances we adopt towards transgressions find
    expression in affective attitudes: from the third person perspective, in
    abhorrence, indignation and contempt, from the perspective of those
    affected, in feelings of violation or resentment towards second persons,
    and from the first person perspective, in shame and guilt. To these correspond
    the positive emotional reactions of admiration, loyalty, gratitude, etc. ...
    [M]oral judgements ... differ from other feelings and evaluations in being
    tied to obligations that function as reasons. We do not regard these utterances
    as expressions of mere sentiments and preferences.' However, the positive
    interpretation of values, common to Habermas and Boudon, should not
    lead to any conclusions as to the ways of accessing ethical truths. Boudon
    basically disagrees with the idea that communicative reason can access that
    kind of truth (see Boudon, 1995a: 299ff.; Boudon, 1999a).

7 'Qu'est-ce en effet qu'une explication scientifique qi ne viserait pas le réalisme?'

8 This would probably be the interpretation given by Steven Lukes, who argues that 'the use of the word "rational" and its cognates has caused untold confusion' and that 'Max Weber is largely responsible for this. His use of these terms is irredeemably opaque and shifting.' (Lukes, 1967: 259).

9 This is the reason why Boudon has, in the last few years, tried to develop a cognitive approach to the problem of rationality. According to him, ' except in simple and marginal cases, action includes theories, conjectures or principles; in other words, ... sociology as well as economics and the other social sciences should develop a more cognitively oriented theory of action.' (Boudon, 1989c: 176). This approach involves the use of categories whose interpretation is basically a hermeneutic problem and cannot be taken in an isolated or general fashion.

10 'Il arrive que le fils ressemble à sa mère, que la mère ressemble à sa propre mère, mais que le petit-fils ne ressemble pas à sa grand-mère.'

11 'X n'avait pas de raisons de croire (de faire) Y, mais...'.

12 '[L]es sciences sociales peuvent se dispenser de donner une rèponse à ces questions ontologiques naïves. Ce qui est vrai, c'est que *certains* comportements, *certaines* actions et *certaines* croyances s'expliquent de façon irrationnelle et d'autres de façon rationnelle.'

13 Boudon recognises the fact that the Weberian notion of *Vestehen* includes emotions and affective states. This is why the model of rationality proposed by him has to leave space for irrationality, despite the limited importance that Boudon attributes to some emotions and affective states in sociological explanation: 'emotions and affective states are *always* at work in behaviour. Thus, the magician who believes that his rituals will bring rain accomplishes them because he (as well as the people to the benefit of whom he operates) *fears* that rain does not fall. This fear need hardly to be accounted for, however. Anyone can understand it: no sociologist is needed at this point' (Boudon, 1993d: 90).

14 'On peut ... facilement conclure que le "désenchantement" – au sens de l'évanouissement de la croyance en la transcendance – conduit inévitablement à l'anarchie polythéiste de valeurs: si les valeurs n'ont pas de réalité extérieure, elles ne sont plus de valeurs; or, l'extinction de la transcendance est indissociablement celle de l'exteriorité des valeurs; l'extinction de la transcendance implique don celle des valeurs. Mais ce syllogisme confond en réalité les modalités de la représentation des valeurs avec les valeurs elle-mêmes.'

15 For a justification of this substitution, see Chapter 2.

16 This is in fact the core of Boudon's critique of Rawls' theory of justice. Although Boudon (1995a) believes that the contractualist method developed by Rawls is fruitful and legitimate, his theory of justice as fairness is not as comprehensive as Rawls claimed it to be (despite the less universalistic ambitions of his second book). First, because it bears only a political, not a metaphysical or even moral, dimension. Second, because, even as a political

theory, it overlooks the fact that the feelings of legitimacy generated by inequalities cannot be perceived only from the perspective of the distribution of goods. One has also to consider how these goods are constituted and what are the more or less tacit ends to which they contribute. And this can only be done in terms of concrete systems of interaction. A formal definition of justice in terms of an abstract and indeterminate society is devoid of any (normative) content. This is not denying the existence of universal principles. According to Boudon (ibid.: 391), their existence is what renders it possible to understand the reasons of actors who belong to different systems of interaction. But it is not possible to analyse feelings of legitimacy or illegitimacy experienced by actors in a situation of inequality if one abstracts the particularities of the system of interaction in which actors are placed.

17   The categorical imperative is: 'Act only according to that maxim by which you can at the same time will that it should become a universal law.' (Kant, 1990: 38).

18   'The ground of obligation ... must not be sought in the nature of man or in the circumstances in which he is placed but *a priori* solely in the concepts of pure reason, and ... every precept which rests on principles of mere experience, even a precept which is in certain respects universal, so far as it leans in the least on empirical grounds (perhaps only in regard to the motive involved) may be called a practical rule but never a moral law.' (Kant, 1990: 5).

19   '... un trait fondamental de la nature humaine. Il en résulte qu'une idée supérieure à une outre d'un point de vue rationnel est par là même dotée d'une force intrinsèque.'

4   Understanding, explanation and objectivity

1   The 'Neo-Marxists' Boudon refers to are, according to a text of the same period (Boudon and Bourricaud, 1982: 580–3), Althusser and Balibar.

2   '[L'interprétation] a une fonction heuristique et aussi une fonction d'intelligibilité'.

3   '[L]a notion de compreéhension s'applique exclusivement ... à l'óperation de projection par laquelle l'acteur analyse le comportement, l'attitude ou les actes de tel individu. Car la compréhension est toujours compréhension de l'acteur individuel. Une action individuelle peut être comprise; un comportement collectif doit être expliqué.'

4   'Il arrive en effet bien souvent que plusieurs explications différéntes d'un même phénomène puissent être consideréées comme vrais.'

5   The notation [ ]* is used to call the reader's attention to the use of the a priori notion in question.

6   '(1) Tel phénomène P peut donner lieu à des interprétations multiples;
(2) L'on ne peut montrer que l'une de ces interprétations est objectivement préférable aux autres;
(3) [La vérité est unique]*
(4) Il est illusoire de parler de vérité à propos des interprétations de P;

(5) L'intérêt d'une interprétation particulière de P ne peut, dans ce cas, reposer sur as valeur de vérité;

(6) Il doit donc émaner de ce qu'elle exprime d'autres valeurs (par example des valeurs *esthétiques*).'

7 For a realist interpretation of Kant which sharply contrasts with Boudon's neo-Kantianism, see Beyleveld (1980).

8 '1)[Q a *une* cause]*

2) Quelle est la cause de Q?

3) [Une cause *réelle* possède la propriété S]*

4) P a la propriété S

5) P est *une* cause *réelle* de Q

---

6) P est *la* cause de Q.'

9 'Certaines de ces structures amplifient les objectifs des agents, d'autres les retounent, certaines les respectent mais produisent des effets différés indésirables. Certaines produisent des états collectifs de tension ne resultant pas de l'antagonisme des intérêts. D'autres produisent indirectement des effets collectivement positifs que les agents sereient incapables de réaliser s'ils cherchaitent à les obtenir directement. D'autres encore sont responsables de changements sociaux globaux prenent la forme de véritables innovations collectives.'

10 'La manie de vouloir absolument trouver des "lois" de la vie sociale ... est simplement un retour au credo philosophique des anciens métaphysiciens selon lequel toute connaissance doit être absolument universelle et nécessaire.'

11 This notion of necessity has to be distinguished from the one used to refer to natural and logical necessity: whereas the latter refers to the intrinsic (material or logical) relations between a cause and its effect, the former refers to the conditions (event, state, phenomenon, or process) which are necessary, i.e. which have to happen, in order that another event follows it.

12 Mental states are, for Davidson, events which involve propositional attitudes such as 'believing, hoping, expecting, fearing ... that' (Passmore, 1985: 67).

13 This means that, for Elster, a causal account of intentional explanation involves a very thin notion of rationality according to which beliefs and desires have to be consistent.

14 Elster does not hold that the explanation of beliefs and desires should always be a causal one: there are intentional explanations of belief formation which can account for these beliefs and desires, pushing the need for causal explanation further back. An example of intentional explanation of desires would be through 'character planning' (Elster, 1983: 83–4).

Bibliography

Antisseri, D.; Pellicani, L. (1992) *L'Individualismo Metodologico: Una Polemica sul Mestiere Dello Scienziato Sociale*. Milan: Franco Angeli.

Archer, M.S. (1995) *Realist Social Theory: The Morphogenetic Approach*. Cambridge: Cambridge University Press.

Baert, P. (1995) 'O Realismo Crítico e as Ciências Sociais'. *Dados*, Vol. 38, No. 2.

Baker, E. (1960) *Social Contract: Essays by Locke, Hume and Rousseau*. Oxford: Oxford University Press.

Becker, G. (1986) 'The Economic Approach to Human Behaviour', in J. Elster (ed.) *Rational Choice: Readings in Social and Political Theory*. Oxford: Basil Blackwell.

Bell, D. (1998) 'Introduction', in D. Schnapper *Community of Citizens: On the Modern Idea of Nationality*. New Brunswick: Transaction Publishers.

Benton, T. (1977) *Philosophical Foundations of the Three Sociologies*. London: Routledge & Kegan Paul.

—— (1981) 'Realism and Social Science: Some Comments on Roy Bhaskar's "The Possibility of Naturalism" '. *Radical Philosophy*, No. 27.

Beyleveld, D. (1980) 'Transcendentalism and Realism'. Unpublished paper presented at a conference of the Theory Group of the British Sociological Association. University of Sussex.

Bhargava, R. (1992) *Individualism in Social Sciences: Forms and Limits of a Methodology*. Oxford: Clarendon Press.

Bhaskar, R. (1979) *The Possibility of Naturalism: A Philosophical Critique of the Contemporary Human Sciences*. Brighton: The Harvester Press.

—— (1989) *Reclaiming Reality: A Critical Introduction to Contemporary Philosophy*. London: Verso.

—— (1991) *Philosophy and the Idea of Freedom*. Oxford: Basil Blackwell.

—— (1997) *A Realist Theory of Science*, 2nd edn. London: Verso.

—— (1998) 'General Introduction', in M. Archer *et al.* (eds) *Critical Realism: Essential Readings*. London: Routledge.

Blegvad, M. (1979) 'Un-French', in R. Boudon *La Logique du Social: Introduction a L'Analyse Sociologique*. Paris: Hachette.

Boudon, R. (1968) *A Quoi Sert la Notion de 'Structure'?: Essai sur la Signification de Structure dans les Sciences Humaines*. Paris: Gallimard.

—— (1972) 'On the Underlying Epistemology of Some Sociological Theories and on its Scientific Consequences'. *Synthèse*, No. 24.

—— (1974) *Education, Opportunity and Social Inequality: Changing Prospects in Western Society*. New York: Wiley/Interscience.

—— (1979) *La Logique du Social: Introduction a L'Analyse Sociologique*. Paris: Hachette.

—— (1980) *The Crisis in Sociology: Problems of Sociological Epistemology*. London: Macmillan.

—— (1981) 'Undesired Consequences and Types of Structures of Inter-dependence', in P. Blau; R. Merton (eds.) *Continuities in Structural Inquiry*. London: Sage.

—— (1982) *The Unintended Consequences of Social Action*. London: Macmillan.

—— (1983) 'Progrès Récents de la Théorie Sociologique'. *Revue des Sciences Morales et Politiques*, Vol. 138, No. 2.

—— (1984) *La Place du Désordre*. Paris: Presses Universitaires de France.

—— (1986a) *L'Ideologie: ou L'Origine des Idées Reçues*. Paris: Fayard.

—— (1986b) 'The Problems of the Philosophy of History'. *Social Science Information*, Vol. 25, No. 4.

—— (1986c) 'Individualisme et Holisme dans les Sciences Sociales', in P. Birnimbaum; J. Leca (eds.) *Sur L'Individualisme: Théories et Méthodes*. Paris: Presses de la Fondation Nationale des Sciences Politiques.

—— (1989a) 'La Théorie de L'Action Sociale de Parsons: La Conserver, mais la Dépasser'. *Sociologie et Sociétés*, Vol. 21, No. 1.

—— (1989b) 'Explication, Interprétation, Idéologie', in A. Jacob (ed.) *Encyclopédie Philosophique Universelle*. Vol. I. *L'Univers Philosophique*. Paris: Presses Universitaires de France.

—— (1989c) 'Subjective Rationality and the Explanation of Social Behaviour'. *Rationality and Society*, Vol. 1, No. 2.

—— (1989d) 'Why do Social Scientists tend to see the World as Over-Ordered?' *Philosophica*, Vol. 44, No. 22.

—— (1990a) *L'Art de se Persuader: Des Idées Douteuses, Fragiles ou Fausses*. Paris: Fayard.

—— (1990b) 'Epistemological Realism', in P. Weingartner; G.J.W. Dorn (eds) *Studies on Mario Bunge's Treatise*. Amsterdam: Rodopi.

—— (1991a) 'On Two Questions: Should Man be Considered as Rational? How to Distinguish Science from Non-Science?'. *New Ideas in Psychology*, Vol. 9, No. 2.

—— (1991b) 'Weber's Notion of Rationality and the Theory of Rationality in Contemporary Social Sciences', in H.J. Helle (ed.) *Verstehen and Pragmatism: Essays in Interpretative Sociology*. Frankfurt: Perter Lang.

—— (1992) 'Explaining Ungrounded Beliefs: Wilhelm Albert Memorial Lecture 1991'. Report 92.4. Oslo: Institute für Samfunnsforskning.

—— (1993a) 'Introduction', in R. Boudon, P. Lazarsfeld (eds) *On Social Research and Its Language*. Chicago: University of Chicago Press.

—— (1993b) 'Between Agency and Social Structure: An Epistemological Point'. *Schweizerische Zeitschrift für Soziologie*, Vol. 19.

—— (1993c) 'Beyond the Alternative Between the Homo Sociologicus and the Homo Oeconomicus: Toward a Theory of Cold Beliefs' in A.B. Soresen; S. Spilerman (eds.) *Social Theory and Social Policy: Essays in Honor of James S. Coleman*. London: Praeger.

—— (1993d) 'More on "Good Reasons": Reply to Critics'. *International Studies in the Philosophy of Science*, Vol. 7, No. 1.

—— (1993e) 'Toward a Synthetic Theory of Rationality'. *International Studies in the Philosophy of Science*, Vol. 7, No. 1.

—— (1994) 'Durkheim et Weber: Convergences de Méthode', in M Hirschhorn; J. Coenen-Huther (eds.) *Durkheim et Weber: Vers la Fin des Malentêndus*. Paris: L'Harmattan.

—— (1995a) *Le Juste et le Vrai: Études sur L'Objectivité des Valeurs et de la Connaissance*. Paris: Fayard.

—— (1995b) 'Should One Still Read Durkheim's Rules After One Hundred Years? Raymond Boudon Interviewed by Massimo Borlandi'. *Revue Suisse de Sociologie*, No. 21, Vol. 3.

—— (1996a) 'The "Rational Choice Model": A Particular Case of the Cognitive Model'. *Rationality and Society*, Vol. 8, No. 2.

—— (1996b) 'Entrevista com Raymond Boudon: Raymond Boudon entrevistado por Cynthia Lins'. *Estudos de Sociologia*, Vol. 2, No. 1.

—— (1996c) 'Porquoi Devenir Sociologue?'. *Revue Française de Science Politique*, Vol. 46, No. 1.

—— (1996d) 'Risposte alle Domande di Enzo Di Nuoscio, in E. Di Nuoscio (ed.) *Le Raggioni degli Individui: L'Individualismo Metodologico di Raymond Boudon*. Rome: Rubbettino Editore.

—— (1997a) 'The Moral Sense'. *International Sociology*, Vol. 12, No. 1.

—— (1997b) "L'Analyse Empirique de L'Action" de Lazarsfeld et la Tradition de la Sociologie Compréhensive' in *Lazarsfeld 1901–1976: La Sociologie de Vienne à New York*. Paris: L'Harmattan.

—— (1998) 'Social Mechanisms Without Black Boxes', in P. Hedström; R. Swedberg (eds.) *Social Mechanisms: An Analytical Approach to Social Theory*. Cambridge: Cambridge University Press.

—— (1999a) *Le Sens de Valeurs*. Paris: Quadrige/Presses Universitaires de France.

—— (1999b) 'Foreword', in M. Bunge (ed.) *The Sociology–Philosophy Connection*. New Brunswick: Transaction Publishers.

—— (2000) 'Le due Sociologie della Conoscenza Scientifica', in R. Boudon; E. Di Nuoscio; C. L Hamlin (eds) *Spegazione Scientifica e Relativismo Culturale*. Rome: LUISS Edizioni.

—— (forthcoming) 'Which Rational Action Theory for the Forthcoming Mainstream Sociology: Methodological Individualism or Rational Choice Theory?' *European Sociological Review*.

Boudon, R.; Bourricaud, F. (1982) *Dictionnaire Critique de la Sociologie*. Paris: Presses Universitaires de France.

Boudon, R.; Lazarsfeld, P.F. (1965) *Le Vocabulaire des Sciences Sociales: Concepts et Indices*. Paris: Mouton/La Haye.

Bouvier, A. (1997) 'Un Paradigme Caché en Sociologie de la Connaissance Scientifique: Le Paradigme Mill-Pareto?'. *Revue Européenne des Sciences Sociales*. Vol. XXXV, No. 118.

Bunge, M. (1999) *The Sociology–Philosophy Connection*. New Brunswick: Transaction Publishers.

Busino, G. (1994) 'Response à Raymond Boudon', in R. Boudon; M. Clavelin (eds) *Le Relativisme est-il Resistable? Regards sur la Sociologie des Sciences*. Actes du Colloque International La Sociologi de la Connaissance Scientifique: Bilan et Perspectives. Paris: Presses Universitaires de France.

Caillé, A. (1988) *Critique de la Raison Utilitaire: Manifeste du MAUSS*. Paris: La Découverte.

Cohn, G. (1993) 'Apresentação', in R. Boudon; F. Bourricaud (eds) *Dicionário Crítico de Sociologia*. São Paulo: Ática.

Collier, A. (1998) 'Realism and Formalism in Ethics', in M. Archer *et al.* (eds) *Critical Realism: Essential Readings*. London: Routledge.

—— (1999) *Being and Worth*. London: Routledge.

Davidson, D. (1980) *Essays on Actions and Events*. Oxford: Clarendon Press.

—— (1984) *Inquiries into Truth and Interpretation*. Oxford: Clarendon Press.

Davidson, W.L. (1957) *Political Thought in England: The Utilitarians from Bentham to Mill*. Oxford: Oxford University Press.

Delanty, G. (1997) *Social Science: Beyond Constructivism and Realism*. Buckingham: Open University Press.

Demeleunaere, P. (1994) *Enquête sur les Principes des Actions Economiques*. PhD thesis, Université de Paris-Sorbonne.

Di Nuoscio, E. (1993) 'L'Individualismo Metodologico nella Sociologia di Raymond Boudon'. *Quaderni del Centro di Metodologia delle Scienze Sociali*. Rome: Libera Universitá Internazionale degli Studi Sociali.

—— (1996) *Le Ragioni degli Individui: L'Individualismo Metodologico di Raymond Boudon*. Soveria Manelli: Rubbetino Editore.

Drouard, A. (1989) 'The Development of Sociology in France after 1945', in N. Genov (ed.) *National Traditions in Sociology*. London: Sage.

Durand, J-P; Weil, R. (1990) *Sociologie Contemporaine*. Paris: Vigot.

Elster, J. (1976) 'Boudon, Education and the Theory of Games'. *Social Science Information*, Vol. 4/5, No. 15,.

—— (1983) *Explaining Technical Change: A Case Study in the Philosophy of Science*. Cambridge: Cambridge University Press.

—— (1986) 'Introduction', in J. Elster (ed.) *Rational Choice: Readings in Social and Political Theory*. Oxford: Basil Blackwell.

—— (1989) *Solomonic Judgements: Studies in the Limitation of Rationality*. Cambridge: Cambridge University Press.

—— (1993) *Ulysses and the Sirens: Studies in Rationality and Irrationality*. London: Cambridge University Press; Paris: Editions de La Maison des Sciences de L'Homme.

Favre, P. (1980) 'Nécessaire mais Non Suffisante: La Sociologie des "Effets Pervers" de Raymond Boudon'. *Revue Française de Science Politique*, Vol. 30, No. 6.

Frey, R.G. (1994) 'Utilitarianism', in W. Outhwaite; T. Bottomore (eds.) *The Blackwell Dictionary of Twentieth-Century Social Thought*. Oxford: Basil Blackwell.

Gadamer, H-G. (1998) *Verdade e Método: Traços Fundamentais de uma Hermenêutica Filosófica*. Petrópolis: Vozes.

Giddens, A. (1979) *Central Problems in Social Theory: Action, Structure and Contradiction in Social Analysis*. London: Macmillan.

—— (1993) *The Constitution of Society: Outline of the Theory of Structuration*. Oxford: Polity Press.

—— (2000) *Mundo em Descontrole: O que a Globalização está Fazendo de nós*. Rio de Janeiro: Record.

Godbout, J.T. (1996) 'Les Bonnes Raisons de Donner'. *Recherches: La Revue du MAUSS*, No. 8.

Goldberg, S.E. (1988) *Two Patterns of Rationality in Freud's Writings*. Tuscaloosa, AL: The University of Alabama Press.

Habermas, J. (1988) *On the Logic of the Social Sciences*. Cambridge: Polity Press.

—— (1996) 'On the Cognitive Content of Morality'. *Proceedings of the Aristotelian Society*, Vol. XCVI, No. 3.

Halfpenny, P. (1982) *Positivism and Sociology: Explaining Social Life*. London: George Allen & Unwin.

—— (1994) 'Explanation', in W. Outhwaite; T. Bottomore (eds.) *The Blackwell Dictionary of Twentieth-Century Social Thought*. Oxford: Basil Blackwell.

Hamlin, C.L. (1998) 'A Hermenêutica Romântica de Wilhelm Dilthey'. *Estudos de Sociologia*, Vol. 2, No. 4.

—— (1999) 'Boudon: Agência, Estrutura e Individualismo Metodológico'. *Lua Nova*, No. 48.

—— (2000a) 'Realismo Crítico: Um Programa de Pesquisa para as Ciências Sociais'. *Dados*, Vol. 43, No. 2.

—— (2000b) 'L'Ontologia Sociale della Teoria della Razionalità Cognitiva: Replica a «La Relatività del Relativismo» di Enzo Di Nuoscio', in R. Boudon; E. Di Nuoscio; C.L. Hamlin (eds) *Spiegazione Scientifica e Relativismo Culturale*. Rome: LUISS Edizioni.

Harré, R. (1984) *As Filosofias da Ciência*. Lisboa: Edições Setenta.

—— (1986) *Varieties of Realism: A Rationale for the Natural Sciences*. London: Basil Blackwell.

Harré, R.; Madden, E.H. (1998) 'Conceptual and Natural Necessity', in M. Archer *et al.* (eds.) *Critical Realism: Essential Readings*. London: Routledge.

Hempel, C.G. (1965) *Aspects of Scientific Explanation and Other Essays in the Philosophy of Science*. New York: The Free Press.

Hobbes, T. (1972) 'De Cive', in D.H. Monro (ed.) *A Guide to British Moralists*. London: Fontana and Collins.

Hollis, M. (1976) *Rational Economic Man: A Philosophical Critique of Neo-Classical Economics*. Cambridge: Cambridge University Press.

—— (1977) *Models of Man: Philosophical Thoughts on Social Action*. Cambridge: Cambridge University Press.

—— (1987) *The Cunning of Reason*. Cambridge: Cambridge University Press.

—— (1994) 'Rationality and Reason', in W. Outhwaite; T. Bottomore (eds) *The Blackwell Dictionary of Twentieth-Century Social Thought*. Oxford: Basil Blackwell.

Hume, D. (1969) [1739] *A Treatise of Human Nature*. E. Mossner (ed.). Harmondsworth: Penguin Books.

James, S. (1984) *The Content of Social Explanation*. Cambridge: Cambridge University Press.

Kant, I. (1990) [1784] *Foundations of the Metaphysics of Morals*. Englewood Cliffs, NJ: Prentice-Hall.

—— (1994) [1781] *Critique of Pure Reason*. London: Everyman

Kendall, P.L. (ed.) (1982) *The Varied Sociology of Paul F. Lazarsfeld*. New York: Columbia University Press.

Layder, D. (1994) *Social Theory*. London: Sage.

Lazarsfeld, P.F. (1993) *On Social Research and Its Language*. R. Boudon (ed.). Chicago: The University of Chicago Press.

Lewis, D.; Smith, R. (1980) *American Sociology and Pragmatism: Mead, Chicago Sociology, and Symbolic Interaction*. Chicago: University of Chicago Press.

Lukes, S. (1967) 'Some Problems about Rationality'. *Archives Européennes de Sociologie*, Vol. VIII, No. 2.

Mandelbaum, M. (1992) 'Societal facts', in J. O'Neill (ed.) *Modes of Individualism and Collectivism*. Hampshire: Gregg Revivals.

Oakes, G. (ed.) (1977) 'Introduction', in M. Weber, *Critique of Stammler*. London: The Free Press.

Outhwaite, W. (1983) *Concept Formation in Social Science*. London: Routledge & Kegan Paul.

—— (1987) *New Philosophies of Social Science: Realism Hermeneutics and Critical Theory*. London: Macmillan.

—— (1994a) *Habermas: A Critical Introduction*. Cambridge: Polity Press.

——(1994b) 'Hans-Georg Gadamer', in Q. Skinner (ed.) *The Return of Grand Theory in the Human Sciences*. Cambridge: Cambridge University Press.

——(1996) 'Social Action and the Production of Society', in J. Clark; M. Diani (eds) *Alain Touraine*. Lewes: Falmer Press.

Papineau, D. (1978) *For Science in the Social Sciences*. London: Macmillan.

Passmore, J. (1985) *Recent Philosophers*. London: Duckworth.

—— (1994) *A Hundred Years of Philosophy*, 4th edn. London: Penguin Books.

Popper, K. (1947) *The Open Society and its Enemies*. Vol. I, *The Spell of Plato*. London: Routledge.

—— (1957) *The Poverty of Historicism*. London: Routledge & Kegan Paul.

—— (1965) *The Logic of Scientific Discovery*. London: Hutchinson.

—— (1979) *Objective Knowledge: An Evolutionary Approach*. Oxford: Clarendon Press.

—— (1983) *Realism and the Aim of Science*. London: Hutchinson.

—— (1994) *Knowledge and the Body/Mind Problem: In Defence of Interaction*. London: Routledge.

Porpora, D. (1998) 'Four Concepts of Social Structure', in M. Archer *et al.* (eds.) *Critical Realism: Essential Readings*. London: Routledge.

Rorty, R. (1989) *Contingency, Irony and Solidarity*. Cambridge: Cambridge University Press.

Sayer, A. (1992) *Method in Social Science: A Realist Approach*. London: Routledge.

Schuurman, F.J. (1994) 'Agency Structure and Globalisation in Development Studies'. *Nijmegen Studies in Development and Cultural Change*, Vol. 21: *Current Issues in Development Studies: Global Aspects of Agency and Structure*. Saarbrucken.

Segady, T.W. (1987) *Values, Neo-Kantianism and the Development of Weberian Methodology*. New York: Peter Lang.

Sen, B.; Williams, B. (1994) 'Introduction: Utilitarianism and Beyond', in B. Sen; B. Williams (eds.) *Utilitarianism and Beyond*. Cambridge: Cambridge University Press; Paris: Editions de la Maison des Sciences de L 'Homme.

Smith, A. (1976) *The Theory of Moral Sentiments*. Indianapolis: Liberty Press/ Liberty Classics.

Stoetzel, J.; Lazarsfeld, P. (1965) 'Définition d'Intention et Espace d'Atributs', in R. Boudon; P.F. Lazarsfeld (eds) *Le Vocabulaire des Sciences Sociales: Concepts et Indices*. Paris: Mouton/ La Haye.

Stokes, G. (1998) *Popper: Philosophy, Politics and Scientific Method*. Cambridge: Polity Press; Oxford: Basil Blackwell.

Touraine, A. (1988) *Return of the Actor: Social Theory in Postindustrial Society*. Minneapolis: University of Minnesota Press.

Watkins, J.W.N. (1952) 'Ideal Types and Historical Explanation in the Social Sciences'. *British Journal of Philosophy*, Vol. VIII, No. 30.

Weber, M. (1977) *Critique of Stammler*. London: The Free Press.

—— (1978) *Economy and Society: An Outline of Interpretive Sociology*. Berkeley: University of California Press.

—— (1992) *Metodologia das Ciências Sociais*, Vol. 1. Campinas: Editora da Unicamp.

Index